GOODSON MUMBA

Innovative Leadership

Driving Change in a Rapidly Evolving World

Copyright © 2024 by Goodson Mumba

All rights reserved. No part of this publication may be reproduced, stored or transmitted in any form or by any means, electronic, mechanical, photocopying, recording, scanning, or otherwise without written permission from the publisher. It is illegal to copy this book, post it to a website, or distribute it by any other means without permission.

First edition

ISBN: 9798335509718

*This book was professionally typeset on Reedsy.
Find out more at reedsy.com*

Contents

Preface		iv
Acknowledgement		vii
Dedication		viii
Disclaimer		ix
1	Chapter 1: Understanding Innovation in Leadership	1
2	Chapter 2: Visionary Thinking and Strategic Planning	24
3	Chapter 3: Building a Culture of Innovation	43
4	Chapter 4: Leading Through Change	58
5	Chapter 5: Leveraging Technology and Innovation	77
6	Chapter 6: Empowering and Inspiring Teams	95
7	Chapter 7: Driving Innovation Through Diversity and...	115
8	Chapter 8: Navigating Global Leadership Challenges	134
9	Chapter 9: Ethical Leadership in a Rapidly Changing World	150
10	Chapter 10: The Future of Leadership: Trends and Predictions	166
About the Author		183

Preface

In an era defined by rapid technological advancements, shifting societal expectations, and unprecedented global challenges, the landscape of leadership is undergoing a profound transformation. The leaders of today and tomorrow must not only navigate these changes but also harness their potential to drive innovation and positive impact within their organizations and communities.

"Innovative Leadership: Driving Change in a Rapidly Evolving World" is a comprehensive guide designed to equip leaders with the insights, strategies, and tools necessary to thrive in this dynamic environment. This book is the culmination of years of research, and a deep understanding of the evolving nature of leadership. It aims to inspire and empower leaders to embrace change, foster innovation, and create a lasting, positive impact.

The journey through this book begins with a foundational understanding of innovation in leadership, exploring historical perspectives, the role of creativity, and the delicate balance between innovation and tradition. From there, we delve into the critical aspects of visionary thinking and strategic planning, emphasizing the importance of crafting compelling visions, aligning organizational goals, and anticipating future trends.

Building a culture of innovation is essential for any organization seeking to thrive in the modern world. This book provides practical guidance on encouraging a growth mindset, fostering open communication and collaboration, and creating a safe space for experimentation and learning from failures. Leadership is not just about managing change but leading through it, and we explore the psychology of change, developing effective change management strategies, and sustaining long-term momentum.

Technology plays an integral role in modern leadership, and we examine the impact of emerging technologies, digital transformation strategies, and the ethical considerations that come with them. Empowering and inspiring teams is another cornerstone of innovative leadership, and this book offers insights into identifying and nurturing talent, building high-performing teams, and celebrating successes.

Diversity and inclusion are not just buzzwords but vital components of innovative leadership. We discuss the business case for diversity, harnessing diverse perspectives, and creating an inclusive environment that fuels innovation. Global leadership challenges are also addressed, with strategies for leading across borders, managing remote teams, and adapting to different regulatory environments.

Ethical leadership is paramount in a rapidly changing world, and this book explores balancing profit with purpose, navigating ethical dilemmas, and building trust and credibility. Finally, we look to the future, examining emerging trends in leadership, the impact of artificial intelligence, and preparing for the workplace of tomorrow.

Throughout this book, you will find real-world case studies, practical examples, and actionable insights from some of the most successful and innovative leaders and organizations around the globe. These stories serve not only as inspiration but as tangible proof of what is possible when leaders commit to driving change and fostering innovation.

"Innovative Leadership: Driving Change in a Rapidly Evolving World" is more than just a guide; it is a call to action for leaders at all levels to embrace the challenges and opportunities of our time. Whether you are a seasoned executive, an aspiring leader, or somewhere in between, this book is designed to provide you with the knowledge, inspiration, and tools needed to lead with confidence and impact.

As you embark on this journey, remember that the future of leadership is not just about navigating change but driving it. It is about being bold, visionary, and innovative. It is about making a difference and leaving a legacy that transcends the present. Together, we can shape the future of leadership and create a world where innovation and positive change are the norms.

Welcome to the future of leadership.

Goodson Mumba

Acknowledgement

I would like to eternally and gratefully acknowledge the Almighty God for the infinite intelligence from His universal mind where we draw from all that we come to know and are yet to know. May I also acknowledge and thank everyone that has played a part in my journey of life in terms of spiritual, moral, emotional and material support.

Dedication

I extend my sincerest gratitude to my beloved wife, Edith Mumba, and our children, Angelina, Lubuto, Letticia, Lulumbi, and Butusho, for their unwavering support and understanding throughout the conception, writing, and eventual publication of this book, despite the sacrifices and challenges they endured.

Disclaimer

This book is a work of fiction. Names, characters, businesses, places, events, and incidents are either the products of the author's imagination or used in a fictitious manner. Any resemblance to actual persons, living or dead, or actual events is purely coincidental.

1

Chapter 1: Understanding Innovation in Leadership

Defining Innovation: What It Means for Leaders

Alex Carter sat in his sleek, minimalist office on the 20th floor of InovaTech's headquarters, gazing out at the bustling cityscape below. The sun was setting, casting a warm orange glow over the skyscrapers. Despite the serene view, Alex's mind was racing. InovaTech had just suffered a major setback: their highly anticipated AI product launch had been upstaged by a competitor's unexpected breakthrough.

He sighed, turning away from the window to face the whiteboard that dominated one wall of his office. It was covered in diagrams, notes, and ideas, all related to the product that now seemed outdated. Alex knew that to navigate this crisis, he needed to redefine what innovation meant for himself and his company.

"Call a meeting with the leadership team," Alex said to his

assistant over the intercom. "I want everyone in the conference room in an hour."

An hour later, the key members of InovaTech's leadership team were gathered around the large conference table. There was a palpable tension in the air. Alex could see the uncertainty in their eyes—uncertainty that mirrored his own.

"Thank you for coming on such short notice," Alex began, standing at the head of the table. "We all know the situation we're facing. Our competitors have caught us off guard, and our product is no longer the game-changer we thought it was."

He paused, letting his words sink in. "But this setback is also an opportunity. It's a wake-up call. We need to rethink our approach to innovation."

Heads nodded around the table, but Alex could sense the skepticism. He took a deep breath and continued. "Innovation isn't just about creating new products or technologies. It's about changing the way we think, the way we operate, and the way we lead. It's about constantly challenging the status quo and pushing the boundaries of what's possible."

He walked over to the whiteboard and picked up a marker. "Let's start by defining innovation. What does it mean for us as leaders? How do we foster it within our teams and our company?"

Sarah, the head of product development, spoke up first. "Innovation means staying ahead of the curve, anticipating market needs before they arise."

"Absolutely," Alex agreed, writing 'Anticipate Market Needs' on the whiteboard. "What else?"

"It's about taking risks," said Mark, the CFO. "Calculated risks that can lead to significant rewards."

Alex nodded, adding 'Calculated Risks' to the list. "Good.

What else?"

"It's about collaboration," said Lisa, the head of HR. "Bringing together diverse perspectives to solve problems in new ways."

"Exactly," Alex said, writing 'Collaboration' on the board. "Innovation thrives in a collaborative environment."

"Flexibility is crucial," added Tom, the COO. "We need to be agile, ready to pivot when necessary."

"Flexibility and agility," Alex echoed, adding those words to the list. "Anything else?"

"Empowerment," said Maria, the head of marketing. "Empowering our employees to think creatively and take initiative."

"Empowerment," Alex repeated, writing it down. "We need to create a culture where every team member feels empowered to contribute ideas and solutions."

The whiteboard now displayed a comprehensive list: Anticipate Market Needs, Calculated Risks, Collaboration, Flexibility and Agility, Empowerment.

"This is our new definition of innovation," Alex said, stepping back. "It's more than just technology or products. It's a mindset, a culture, and a way of leading. If we can embrace these principles, we can turn this setback into a launching pad for even greater success."

The mood in the room began to shift. Faces that had been tense and uncertain now showed signs of determination and hope.

"We're not just going to survive this challenge," Alex continued. "We're going to use it to become stronger and more innovative than ever. Together, we'll lead InovaTech into a new era of success."

As the meeting concluded, Alex felt a renewed sense of purpose. He knew the road ahead would be tough, but he was confident that with a clear vision of innovation and a committed team, they could navigate any obstacle and emerge as true leaders in their rapidly evolving world.

Historical Perspectives on Innovative Leadership

As the team began to disperse, Alex called out, "Hold on, everyone. Before we go any further, I think it's crucial that we look back at some historical perspectives on innovative leadership. By understanding how great leaders of the past approached innovation, we can glean valuable lessons for our own journey."

He saw a few surprised faces. History lessons weren't the norm in their fast-paced tech environment, but Alex knew that sometimes, the best insights came from looking backward to move forward.

"Let's reconvene in 15 minutes. I'll need Sarah, Mark, and Lisa to stay behind to help set up," Alex said.

Fifteen minutes later, the leadership team was back in the conference room. This time, Alex had arranged for a projector and screen. The lights dimmed as he began his presentation.

"Today, we're going to explore three historical figures whose innovative leadership changed the world: Thomas Edison, Steve Jobs, and Nelson Mandela. Each of these leaders faced significant challenges and responded with groundbreaking innovation."

The screen lit up with a portrait of Thomas Edison.

Thomas Edison: The Relentless Inventor

"Thomas Edison is often celebrated for his invention of the electric light bulb, but his approach to innovation was much broader. He held over 1,000 patents and believed in constant experimentation. Edison once said, 'I have not failed. I've just found 10,000 ways that won't work.'"

Alex paused, looking around the room. "Edison's lesson for us is the power of persistence and learning from failure. We must create an environment where failure is seen as a step toward success, not a setback."

He clicked to the next slide, showing an image of Steve Jobs.

Steve Jobs: The Visionary Leader

"Steve Jobs, co-founder of Apple, revolutionized multiple industries with his innovative vision. Jobs was known for his intense focus on design and user experience. He once said, 'Innovation distinguishes between a leader and a follower.'"

Alex highlighted a few key products: the iPhone, the iPod, and the MacBook. "Jobs's ability to foresee what customers wanted—sometimes even before they knew it themselves—was unparalleled. He taught us the importance of vision and understanding the market deeply."

The final slide revealed Nelson Mandela.

Nelson Mandela: The Transformative Leader

"Nelson Mandela might seem an unconventional choice for a discussion on innovation, but his leadership during the end of apartheid in South Africa was profoundly innovative. Mandela once said, 'It always seems impossible until it's done.'"

Alex noted Mandela's use of reconciliation and peace to unite a divided nation. "Mandela's approach teaches us about innovative problem-solving and the power of leading with empathy and vision. He showed that true innovation often involves bringing people together in new and unexpected ways."

Drawing Parallels

Alex turned off the projector and faced his team. "So, what can we learn from Edison, Jobs, and Mandela? Persistence, visionary thinking, and empathetic leadership. These principles are timeless."

Sarah raised her hand. "It's fascinating how these leaders' innovations weren't just about their products or immediate goals, but about changing the way people thought and interacted."

"Exactly," Alex agreed. "Innovative leadership is about transforming mindsets and cultures, not just processes and products. As we move forward, we need to embody these lessons. We need to be relentless in our pursuit of new ideas like Edison, visionary like Jobs, and empathetic and unifying like Mandela."

Mark, usually reserved, spoke up next. "It's inspiring. We often get so caught up in the daily grind that we forget the bigger picture. This reminds me that our work can have a lasting impact if we approach it with the right mindset."

Alex nodded. "That's the goal. We're not just building products; we're building a legacy. By understanding and applying these historical perspectives, we can become leaders who drive lasting, positive change in a rapidly evolving world."

As the meeting concluded for the second time, there was a different energy in the room. Alex could see the shift in his team's attitudes. They were not just ready to tackle the next project—they were ready to innovate with a renewed sense of purpose and historical wisdom.

Alex returned to his office, feeling more confident. He knew that this blend of historical insight and modern ambition would be the foundation upon which InovaTech could rebuild and thrive. The journey ahead was clear, and with these lessons from the past, they were prepared to forge a future of unprecedented innovation.

The Role of Creativity in Leadership

After the illuminating session on historical perspectives, Alex Carter could sense a new energy buzzing in the InovaTech office. But he knew that understanding the past was only part of the equation. The next step was to harness the power of creativity within his team.

That evening, Alex decided to shake things up. He sent out a company-wide email inviting everyone to a creative brainstorming session the following morning. The subject line simply read: "Unleash Your Creativity."

The Next Morning

The large open area in InovaTech's office was transformed overnight. Bean bags replaced standard chairs, walls were lined with whiteboards, and tables were scattered with colorful markers, sticky notes, and various prototypes of their products. The smell of fresh coffee filled the air, mingling with the anticipation of something new and exciting.

Alex stood at the center, waiting as employees trickled in, curious and intrigued by the unusual setup. Once everyone was gathered, he began.

"Good morning, InovaTech! Today, we're diving into something fundamental: creativity. Creativity isn't just for artists or designers. It's a crucial element of leadership and innovation. It's about thinking differently and approaching problems in new ways."

He smiled, seeing the excitement on their faces. "Let's start with a quick exercise. I want you to form small groups and use these materials to create a prototype of any product you think could change the world. It doesn't have to be realistic—just let your imagination run wild."

Unleashing Creativity

The room buzzed with activity. Teams quickly formed, and the air was filled with animated discussions and laughter. Alex walked around, observing and occasionally joining in on the creative process. He saw engineers sketching outlandish devices, marketers envisioning futuristic ad campaigns, and developers brainstorming revolutionary software.

One group caught his attention. They were huddled around a table, deeply engrossed in creating a prototype of a device that combined augmented reality with virtual travel experiences. "Imagine if we could travel anywhere in the world without leaving our homes," one of them explained.

Alex nodded, impressed. "This is exactly what I'm talking about. Creativity is about breaking boundaries and imagining what's possible."

The Presentation

After an hour of intense creativity, Alex called everyone to gather around. Each group presented their prototypes, showcasing an array of imaginative ideas: from AI-driven health monitors to interactive educational tools for children. The diversity and ingenuity were astounding.

"Fantastic work, everyone!" Alex exclaimed. "This is the kind of creative thinking that can drive our company forward. But creativity isn't just about wild ideas—it's about applying this mindset to our everyday challenges."

He continued, "Creativity in leadership means looking at problems from different angles, encouraging innovative solutions, and fostering an environment where new ideas can thrive."

Practical Application

To illustrate his point, Alex shared a personal anecdote. "When we first started InovaTech, we faced a massive hurdle: securing initial funding. Traditional investors were skeptical of our unconventional approach. But instead of giving up, we got creative. We hosted a series of tech demos in unusual locations—museums, art galleries, even parks. This not only attracted attention but also allowed potential investors to experience our vision firsthand in unique settings. That creativity paid off and set us on the path we're on today."

He paused, letting the story sink in. "The lesson here is that creativity can be a powerful tool in leadership. It helps us see opportunities where others see obstacles and drives us to find innovative solutions."

Encouraging Continuous Creativity

Alex then outlined a new initiative: the InovaTech Creativity Labs. "Starting today, we're dedicating time each week for creative brainstorming sessions like this one. We'll rotate teams, mix departments, and focus on tackling specific challenges creatively. I want everyone to feel empowered to contribute ideas, no matter how unconventional they might seem."

The announcement was met with enthusiastic applause. Alex could see the spark in his team's eyes—the same spark that had driven him to create InovaTech in the first place.

Conclusion

As the session wrapped up, Alex felt a sense of accomplishment. He had not only reignited the creative spirit within his team but had also highlighted the essential role of creativity in leadership. By fostering an environment that encouraged imaginative thinking and innovative solutions, Alex was confident that InovaTech could navigate any challenge the rapidly evolving tech world threw their way.

Returning to his office, Alex glanced at the sketches and notes scattered across his desk from the morning's activities. He smiled, knowing that the seeds of innovation had been sown, ready to grow and transform into the groundbreaking solutions of tomorrow.

With a renewed sense of purpose and a creative mindset, Alex was ready to lead InovaTech into a future brimming with possibilities.

Innovation vs. Tradition: Finding the Balance

With the spirit of creativity alive and buzzing within InovaTech, Alex Carter knew the next challenge lay in balancing this newfound innovation with the company's established traditions. InovaTech had grown rapidly, and some traditions and practices were deeply ingrained in its culture. Alex needed to ensure that innovation did not erode the company's core values but rather enhanced them.

The Call for Balance

The day after the creative brainstorming session, Alex called a meeting with InovaTech's senior leadership team. This time, the atmosphere was more formal. The leaders sat around the conference table, curiosity mixed with a bit of apprehension on their faces.

Alex began, "Yesterday was a fantastic display of our collective creativity. But as we push forward with new ideas, we must remember that innovation and tradition are not mutually exclusive. They can and should complement each other."

He paused, seeing some nods of agreement. "We need to find the balance. Our traditions are the foundation upon which we've built this company. They give us our identity and guide our values. But to stay competitive, we also need to innovate continually."

A Real-Life Example

Alex glanced at Mark, the CFO. "Mark, could you share the story of our initial financial strategy and how it has evolved?"

Mark nodded, standing up. "Sure. When we first started, our financial strategy was very conservative. We saved aggressively, avoided debt, and only invested in low-risk opportunities. This approach gave us stability and helped us weather early challenges."

He continued, "However, as we grew, we realized that being too conservative was holding us back. We needed to take calculated risks to expand. We began to invest in high-potential startups and cutting-edge technology. This shift didn't mean abandoning our conservative roots but rather adapting them to our new reality. We kept our careful approach to analysis and due diligence, which is our tradition, while embracing a more aggressive investment strategy."

Alex turned to the team. "This is a perfect example of balancing innovation with tradition. We maintained our core value of financial prudence while evolving our strategy to include innovative investments."

The Workshop

To illustrate this balance further, Alex had planned a hands-on workshop. The team moved to a larger room where two large boards were set up: one labeled "Tradition" and the other "Innovation." The room was filled with sticky notes, markers, and large sheets of paper.

"Let's break into groups," Alex instructed. "I want each group to identify one traditional practice at InovaTech and brainstorm how we can innovate within that framework without losing its core value."

The Brainstorming

The room buzzed with activity as the leaders grouped up and started discussing. After about an hour, the groups reconvened to present their ideas.

The first group focused on InovaTech's customer service tradition. "Our tradition of exceptional customer service is a cornerstone of our company," Sarah began. "But we can enhance it by integrating AI-driven customer support systems that provide instant responses to common queries while still maintaining the personal touch for complex issues."

The next group tackled the company's hiring practices. "We have a tradition of hiring from top-tier universities," Mark said. "While this has served us well, we propose expanding our recruitment to include coding bootcamps and tech meetups. This way, we can tap into a broader talent pool and bring in diverse perspectives, which is crucial for innovation."

Another group addressed the tradition of in-person meetings. "We value face-to-face interactions," Lisa explained. "But with our global expansion, we need to innovate. We propose adopting virtual reality meetings, which can simulate in-person interactions while saving time and travel costs."

Reflection and Implementation

After all the groups presented, Alex stood before the boards. "These are excellent examples of how we can innovate while honoring our traditions. Innovation doesn't mean discarding our values. It means evolving and enhancing them."

He continued, "Starting today, we will implement these ideas. Each of you will lead a small team to develop a detailed plan for integrating these innovations into our traditional practices. We'll review progress in our next leadership meeting."

Conclusion

The meeting concluded with a sense of accomplishment and clarity. Alex felt confident that InovaTech could achieve a harmonious balance between innovation and tradition. By respecting their roots while embracing the future, they would create a robust, dynamic, and forward-thinking organization.

Back in his office, Alex looked at the feedback from the session and felt a deep sense of satisfaction. The balance between innovation and tradition wasn't just a strategic move—it was a philosophy that would guide InovaTech to sustained success. With this balanced approach, Alex was more determined than ever to lead his company through the evolving landscape of the tech world.

As he reflected on the day's discussions, Alex knew that this balance would be the cornerstone of InovaTech's journey forward, ensuring that they remained true to their values while continuously pushing the boundaries of what was possible.

Case Studies of Successful Innovative Leaders

After laying the foundation of balancing innovation with tradition, Alex Carter knew that concrete examples of successful innovative leaders would provide his team with the inspiration and insights they needed. He decided to present case studies of three real-life leaders whose innovative approaches had left indelible marks on their industries.

The Case Studies Session

The leadership team gathered once more in the conference room, this time with an air of eager anticipation. The atmosphere was a mix of curiosity and excitement as they awaited Alex's next lesson.

Alex began, "Today, we're going to look at some of the most influential innovative leaders of our time: Elon Musk, Indra Nooyi, and Reed Hastings. Each of these leaders faced significant challenges and responded with groundbreaking innovation."

He dimmed the lights and started the presentation.

Elon Musk: The Visionary Disruptor

The screen showed an image of Elon Musk, the CEO of SpaceX and Tesla.

"Elon Musk is known for his audacious goals and ability to turn science fiction into reality," Alex started. "From revolutionizing the automotive industry with electric cars to advancing space exploration, Musk exemplifies how bold vision and relentless pursuit can lead to incredible innovation."

Alex highlighted key moments, such as the launch of the first reusable rocket by SpaceX and Tesla's introduction of the Model S. "Musk's willingness to tackle seemingly impossible challenges and his ability to inspire his teams to do the same is a powerful lesson for us. He shows that when you combine ambition with relentless execution, the sky is literally not the limit."

Indra Nooyi: The Transformative Strategist

The next slide featured Indra Nooyi, former CEO of PepsiCo.

"Indra Nooyi transformed PepsiCo by integrating health and sustainability into the company's strategy," Alex continued. "She recognized early on the shifting consumer preferences towards healthier options and led the company through a strategic shift that prioritized 'performance with purpose.'"

He detailed Nooyi's initiatives, such as reducing the sugar content in Pepsi's beverages and expanding the company's portfolio to include more nutritious products. "Nooyi's innovative leadership was about seeing beyond immediate profits to long-term sustainability and consumer well-being. She teaches us the importance of aligning business goals with broader social trends and values."

Reed Hastings: The Entertainment Revolutionary

The final slide showed Reed Hastings, co-founder and CEO of Netflix.

"Reed Hastings revolutionized the entertainment industry by transitioning Netflix from a DVD rental service to a streaming giant," Alex explained. "His foresight in recognizing the potential of streaming technology and his willingness to pivot the company's entire business model is a masterclass in innovation."

He recounted the key moments of Netflix's evolution, from the introduction of the streaming service to the company's investment in original content. "Hastings's ability to disrupt the industry and stay ahead of competitors by continuously innovating is a crucial lesson. He shows us that adaptability and a forward-thinking mindset are essential for sustained success."

The Discussion

Alex turned off the projector and faced his team. "So, what can we learn from Musk, Nooyi, and Hastings?"

Sarah spoke first. "Musk's example shows us the power of having a bold vision and the courage to pursue it, no matter how difficult it seems."

Mark added, "Nooyi's focus on aligning business with social values is crucial. It's about seeing the bigger picture and understanding that innovation can drive both profit and positive change."

Lisa chimed in, "Hastings's ability to pivot and adapt reminds us that innovation often requires us to rethink our entire business model. We need to be willing to take risks and embrace change."

Alex nodded, pleased with the insights. "Exactly. These leaders teach us that innovation is multifaceted. It involves vision, alignment with broader trends, and adaptability. By studying their approaches, we can better understand how to apply these principles to our own leadership."

Applying the Lessons

To ensure these lessons were not just theoretical, Alex proposed a new initiative. "We're going to start a 'Leadership Innovation Program,' where each of you will take turns leading a project inspired by one of these leaders. Whether it's launching a bold new initiative, aligning a project with social values, or pivoting an existing strategy, you'll apply these lessons to drive innovation within your teams."

The team responded enthusiastically, eager to put these insights into practice. Alex could see the excitement in their eyes, a clear indication that these case studies had struck a chord.

Conclusion

As the session wrapped up, Alex felt a deep sense of accomplishment. By studying the successes of Musk, Nooyi, and Hastings, he had provided his team with concrete examples of how innovative leadership could transform industries and inspire significant change.

Returning to his office, Alex reflected on the day's discussions. He was confident that these case studies would serve as valuable guides for InovaTech's leaders, helping them navigate the challenges of a rapidly evolving world with creativity, courage, and strategic foresight.

With these real-life examples of innovative leadership, Alex knew that InovaTech was well on its way to becoming a beacon of innovation, driven by leaders who were not afraid to dream big, adapt to change, and align their goals with a greater purpose.

Common Barriers to Innovation and How to Overcome Them

The momentum at InovaTech was building. The team was energized by the historical perspectives, inspired by the creative brainstorming, and motivated by the case studies of successful leaders. But Alex Carter knew that enthusiasm alone wasn't enough. Innovation faced numerous barriers, and addressing them head-on was crucial.

The Reality Check

At the next meeting, Alex gathered the team in the same conference room where their journey into innovative leadership had begun. The atmosphere was different this time—more serious and reflective.

"Today, we need to confront the barriers that stand in the way of innovation," Alex began, his tone firm but encouraging. "Every company faces obstacles, but true leaders find ways to overcome them."

He clicked to the first slide on the projector, which read, "Common Barriers to Innovation."

Barrier 1: Fear of Failure

"Let's start with the most common barrier: fear of failure," Alex said. "Many of us are afraid to take risks because we fear the consequences of failing. But as we've learned from leaders like Edison and Musk, failure is often a crucial step on the path to success."

He shared a personal anecdote. "When we first launched

InovaTech, our initial product flopped. We were devastated. But instead of giving up, we analyzed what went wrong, learned from our mistakes, and came back stronger with a better product. That failure taught us invaluable lessons and ultimately led to our first major success."

Mark, the CFO, nodded. "It's about changing our mindset. We need to see failure as an opportunity to learn and grow, not as a final verdict."

Barrier 2: Resistance to Change

The next slide read, "Resistance to Change."

"People are naturally resistant to change, especially when they're comfortable with the status quo," Alex continued. "But in a rapidly evolving world, clinging to old ways can be detrimental."

He paused, letting his words sink in. "To overcome this, we need to create a culture that embraces change. This means constant communication about why change is necessary and how it benefits everyone."

Lisa, the head of HR, added, "We can also provide training and support to help employees adapt to new technologies and processes. When people feel equipped to handle change, they're less likely to resist it."

Barrier 3: Lack of Resources

"Next, let's talk about the lack of resources," Alex said, clicking to the next slide. "Innovation often requires significant investment in time, money, and talent. When resources are limited, it's easy to feel stuck."

He looked at Sarah, the head of product development. "Sarah, can you share how we managed resource constraints during the development of our latest product?"

Sarah stood up. "We faced significant budget cuts halfway through the project. Instead of halting progress, we got creative. We formed cross-functional teams to maximize our internal talent and leveraged partnerships with startups that had the technology we needed. This not only saved costs but also accelerated our development process."

"Great example, Sarah," Alex said. "The key is to be resourceful and look for innovative solutions to resource constraints."

Barrier 4: Organizational Silos

The next barrier was displayed on the screen: "Organizational Silos."

"Silos within an organization can stifle innovation by preventing the free flow of ideas and collaboration," Alex explained. "We need to break down these barriers and encourage cross-departmental teamwork."

He shared another story. "A few years ago, our marketing and product development teams barely interacted. This led to misaligned goals and missed opportunities. We introduced regular cross-departmental meetings and collaborative projects, which have since fostered a more unified approach to innovation."

Barrier 5: Short-term Focus

The following slide read, "Short-term Focus."

"Many companies prioritize short-term gains over long-term innovation," Alex said. "While immediate results are important, we must also invest in future-oriented projects."

Mark spoke up, "Our shift towards long-term strategic planning has been beneficial. By setting aside a portion of our budget for R&D and encouraging long-term projects, we've been able to explore new technologies and markets without the pressure of immediate returns."

Barrier 6: Inadequate Leadership

The final barrier appeared on the screen: "Inadequate Leadership."

"Innovative leadership is essential for fostering an innovative culture," Alex concluded. "Leaders must be willing to take risks, support their teams, and drive the vision forward."

He turned to his team. "That's why we're focusing so much on developing our leadership skills. By learning from history, fostering creativity, balancing innovation with tradition, and studying successful leaders, we're equipping ourselves to lead InovaTech into the future."

Overcoming Barriers Together

Alex wrapped up the session with a powerful message. "We've identified the barriers, but more importantly, we've discussed ways to overcome them. Let's commit to applying these strategies. Together, we can turn obstacles into opportunities."

The team left the room with a clear understanding of the challenges ahead and a renewed determination to overcome them. Alex felt a deep sense of satisfaction, knowing that InovaTech's leaders were now equipped to navigate the complexities of innovation.

As he returned to his office, Alex reflected on the journey so far. Addressing these barriers was not just about tackling immediate challenges but about laying the groundwork for a culture of continuous innovation. With this foundation, InovaTech was ready to thrive in a rapidly evolving world, turning every obstacle into a stepping stone towards greater success.

2

Chapter 2: Visionary Thinking and Strategic Planning

Crafting a Compelling Vision

The meeting room buzzed with anticipation as InovaTech's leadership team gathered for the next phase of their journey. Alex Carter, their inspiring CEO, stood at the front of the room, ready to guide them through one of the most critical aspects of leadership: crafting a compelling vision.

Setting the Stage

"Good morning, everyone," Alex began, his voice full of energy. "Today, we're diving into the heart of visionary thinking: crafting a compelling vision. A clear and compelling vision is the foundation upon which great companies are built. It's what guides us, motivates us, and aligns our efforts."

He clicked to the first slide, which displayed the quote, "The best way to predict the future is to create it."

"Peter Drucker's words couldn't be more true," Alex continued. "As leaders, it's our responsibility to envision the future and then set the course to make it a reality."

The Power of a Compelling Vision

Alex paused, scanning the room to ensure he had everyone's full attention. "But what makes a vision compelling? It's not just about having lofty goals. A compelling vision is clear, inspiring, and aligned with our core values. It needs to resonate with every member of the team and give them a sense of purpose."

He shared an anecdote from InovaTech's early days. "When we started InovaTech, our vision was simple yet powerful: 'To create technology that makes life easier for everyone.' This vision wasn't about specific products or technologies; it was about the impact we wanted to have on the world. It inspired us, guided our decisions, and attracted people who shared our passion."

Crafting InovaTech's New Vision

Alex knew it was time for InovaTech to refresh its vision. The company had grown and evolved, and so too should its vision. He decided to engage the leadership team in this crucial task.

"Let's craft a new vision together," Alex proposed. "A vision that reflects who we are today and where we want to go. We'll start with a brainstorming session. Think about what makes InovaTech unique, what we're passionate about, and the impact we want to have on the world."

The team split into smaller groups, each equipped with

whiteboards and markers. The room filled with animated discussions as they explored their ideas. Alex moved from group to group, offering guidance and encouragement.

Group Presentations

After an hour of intense brainstorming, the groups reconvened to present their ideas. The first group's vision focused on technological innovation: "To lead the way in developing groundbreaking technologies that transform industries and improve lives."

The second group emphasized social impact: "To empower communities through technology, making the world more connected, inclusive, and sustainable."

The third group combined both elements: "To innovate with purpose, creating technology that not only advances industries but also enhances everyday life for people around the globe."

Alex listened intently to each presentation, impressed by the passion and creativity on display. "These are all fantastic visions," he said. "Now, let's work together to refine and combine these ideas into a single, compelling vision."

Crafting the Unified Vision

The team dove back into discussion, building on each other's ideas and finding common ground. After another hour of collaboration, they emerged with a unified vision:

"To innovate with purpose, creating technology that transforms industries and enhances everyday life, while empowering communities and fostering a more connected, inclusive, and sustainable world."

Alex wrote the vision on the board and stepped back. "This is our new vision. It's clear, inspiring, and aligned with our core values. It speaks to our passion for innovation, our commitment to social impact, and our desire to make a positive difference in the world."

Communicating the Vision

"Crafting the vision is just the first step," Alex continued. "The next step is to communicate it effectively. We need every member of InovaTech to understand and embrace this vision. It should guide their daily work and inspire them to strive for excellence."

He outlined the communication strategy: a company-wide meeting to introduce the new vision, followed by departmental workshops to discuss how each team's work contributes to this vision. They would also create visual reminders throughout the office and include the vision in all internal and external communications.

Conclusion

As the meeting wrapped up, Alex felt a deep sense of accomplishment. The new vision was not just a statement—it was a commitment to a shared future, a beacon that would guide InovaTech through the challenges and opportunities ahead.

"Remember, a compelling vision is not just words on a page," Alex concluded. "It's a living, breathing part of our culture. Let's bring this vision to life in everything we do, and together, we'll create a future we can all be proud of."

The team left the room with renewed energy and a clear

sense of direction. Alex returned to his office, confident that this new vision would be the driving force behind InovaTech's continued success and innovation.

With this compelling vision in place, InovaTech was ready to embark on the next chapter of its journey, poised to lead with purpose and transform the world through technology.

Aligning Vision with Organizational Goals

With InovaTech's new vision crafted and embraced, Alex Carter knew that the next crucial step was to align this vision with the company's organizational goals. A compelling vision was only effective if it guided every aspect of the organization's strategy and operations.

Mapping the Path Forward

In the conference room, the leadership team gathered once again, their focus now on translating the visionary aspirations into actionable goals.

"Good morning, everyone," Alex greeted, projecting the newly crafted vision onto the screen. "Our vision is ambitious and inspiring, but now we need to ensure that it guides our day-to-day decisions and actions. That's where aligning our vision with organizational goals comes in."

Defining Clear Objectives

Alex divided the team into smaller groups, each tasked with defining specific objectives that would contribute to the realization of the company's vision.

"Think about what each department can do to bring our vision to life," Alex instructed. "These objectives should be clear, measurable, and directly aligned with our overarching vision."

Presenting the Objectives

After an hour of brainstorming and discussion, the groups reconvened to present their proposed objectives.

The first group, representing product development, outlined their objectives to focus on research and development of innovative technologies that address societal challenges while maintaining a competitive edge in the market.

The second group, from marketing and sales, proposed objectives to strengthen brand awareness, expand market reach, and communicate the company's commitment to social impact and innovation.

The third group, comprised of operations and HR, highlighted objectives to optimize internal processes, foster a culture of innovation and diversity, and ensure alignment between the company's vision and employee development programs.

Integrating Objectives into the Strategic Plan

Alex listened attentively to each presentation, taking notes as he considered how to integrate these objectives into InovaTech's strategic plan.

"These objectives are impressive," Alex acknowledged, "and they align well with our vision. Now, let's map out a strategic plan that outlines how we will achieve these goals."

Mapping out the Plan

Together, the leadership team began to map out a strategic plan, identifying key initiatives, timelines, and responsible parties for each objective. They discussed resource allocation, potential challenges, and strategies for measuring progress.

As the plan took shape, Alex could feel the energy in the room. The team was fully engaged, united in their commitment to bringing the company's vision to life.

Reaffirming the Vision

Before concluding the meeting, Alex took a moment to reaffirm the importance of their shared vision.

"Our vision is not just a statement—it's our North Star," he emphasized. "As we move forward, let's keep it at the forefront of everything we do. Let's use it to guide our decisions, motivate our teams, and measure our progress. Together, we will turn this vision into reality."

Conclusion

As the meeting adjourned, the leadership team left the room with a renewed sense of purpose and clarity. They were eager to begin executing the strategic plan and driving InovaTech towards its visionary future.

Alex lingered in the conference room for a moment, reflecting on the progress they had made. With their vision firmly aligned with their organizational goals, he knew that InovaTech was well-positioned to achieve greatness.

With determination and a clear roadmap ahead, InovaTech

was ready to embark on the next phase of its journey, propelled by its compelling vision and unified purpose.

Strategic Foresight: Anticipating Future Trends

With the vision aligned with organizational goals, Alex Carter understood the importance of strategic foresight in navigating the ever-evolving landscape of the tech industry. Anticipating future trends was essential to staying ahead of the competition and realizing InovaTech's ambitious vision.

The Quest for Strategic Foresight

In the boardroom adorned with graphs and charts displaying market trends, Alex gathered the leadership team once more. Today's focus: strategic foresight.

"Good morning, everyone," Alex greeted, his tone serious yet determined. "As we pursue our vision, we must look beyond the present and anticipate future trends that will shape our industry. Strategic foresight is about understanding where the world is headed and positioning ourselves to thrive in that future."

Analyzing Market Trends

The room buzzed with anticipation as Alex led the team through an analysis of current market trends and emerging technologies.

"Artificial intelligence, blockchain, sustainability—these are just a few of the trends shaping the tech industry," Alex explained, pointing to the graphs on the screen. "We need to understand how these trends will impact our business and identify opportunities for innovation."

Predicting Consumer Behavior

Next, Alex turned to consumer behavior, highlighting the importance of predicting and adapting to changing preferences.

"Our customers are at the heart of everything we do," Alex emphasized. "By understanding their needs, desires, and behaviors, we can develop products and services that anticipate their future demands."

Scenario Planning

To illustrate the importance of strategic foresight, Alex introduced the concept of scenario planning.

"We can't predict the future with certainty," Alex acknowledged. "But we can prepare for various possibilities by creating scenarios and developing strategies to address each one."

He divided the team into groups and tasked them with creating scenarios based on different future trends and potential disruptions.

Developing Future-Ready Strategies

After intense brainstorming and analysis, the groups reconvened to present their scenarios and proposed strategies.

One group focused on the rise of decentralized technologies like blockchain, proposing strategies to integrate blockchain into InovaTech's products and services to enhance security and transparency.

Another group addressed the growing demand for sustainable solutions, recommending initiatives to reduce the company's carbon footprint and develop eco-friendly products.

Embracing Innovation and Adaptability

As the presentations concluded, Alex underscored the importance of embracing innovation and adaptability in the face of uncertainty.

"The future is unpredictable," Alex admitted, "but by staying vigilant, adaptive, and forward-thinking, we can navigate whatever challenges and opportunities lie ahead."

Conclusion

As the meeting drew to a close, the leadership team left the boardroom with a renewed sense of purpose and determination. Armed with strategic foresight, they were ready to anticipate future trends, innovate boldly, and lead InovaTech into a future brimming with possibilities.

Alex remained in the boardroom, contemplating the discussions and insights shared. With their vision, goals, and strategies aligned, he knew that InovaTech was well-prepared to seize the opportunities of tomorrow and continue its journey towards greatness.

With strategic foresight as their guiding light, InovaTech was poised to shape the future of the tech industry and make their visionary aspirations a reality.

Developing a Roadmap for Innovation

With the foundation laid for strategic foresight, Alex Carter recognized the importance of developing a roadmap for innovation—a clear path to transform vision into reality. Mapping out this roadmap would guide InovaTech in navigating the complexities of the tech industry and achieving their ambitious goals.

Setting the Stage

In the spacious innovation lab, Alex convened the leadership team once again, this time with a focus on developing a roadmap for innovation.

"Welcome, everyone," Alex greeted, his voice echoing in the vibrant room filled with prototypes and whiteboards. "Today, we're charting our course for innovation—a roadmap that will guide us in turning our vision into tangible results."

Defining Innovation Pillars

Alex began by outlining the key pillars of innovation that would drive the roadmap forward.

"Innovation is more than just developing new products," Alex explained. "It's about reimagining processes, fostering a culture of creativity, and embracing emerging technologies."

He divided the team into groups and tasked each with defining specific areas of innovation, from product development to operational efficiency to customer experience.

Mapping out Initiatives

With the pillars of innovation defined, the groups delved into brainstorming initiatives that would bring these pillars to life.

One group focused on product innovation, proposing initiatives to research and develop groundbreaking technologies that address unmet needs in the market.

Another group addressed process innovation, recommending initiatives to streamline internal workflows and optimize resource allocation.

Integrating Innovation into the Strategic Plan

As the groups presented their proposed initiatives, Alex listened intently, taking notes on how to integrate these ideas into InovaTech's strategic plan.

"These initiatives are the building blocks of our roadmap for innovation," Alex acknowledged. "Now, let's map out a timeline, allocate resources, and define clear metrics for success."

Mapping out the Plan

Together, the leadership team began to map out the roadmap for innovation, identifying key milestones, timelines, and responsible parties for each initiative. They discussed potential challenges, resource constraints, and strategies for overcoming obstacles.

As the roadmap took shape, Alex could feel the excitement in the room. The team was fully engaged, united in their commitment to driving innovation and realizing InovaTech's visionary aspirations.

Reaffirming the Commitment to Innovation

Before concluding the meeting, Alex took a moment to reaffirm the importance of their commitment to innovation.

"Our roadmap for innovation is not just a document—it's a promise to ourselves and our customers," Alex emphasized. "Let's use it to guide our actions, inspire our teams, and propel InovaTech to new heights of success."

Conclusion

As the meeting adjourned, the leadership team left the innovation lab with a renewed sense of purpose and determination. They were eager to begin executing the roadmap for innovation and bringing InovaTech's vision to life.

Alex remained in the lab, surrounded by the energy of creativity and innovation. With their roadmap in hand, he knew that InovaTech was well-equipped to navigate the challenges and opportunities ahead, poised to lead the tech industry into a future filled with possibility.

Communicating the Vision Effectively

With the roadmap for innovation charted, Alex Carter understood the importance of effectively communicating the company's vision to every member of the organization. Clear and consistent communication would ensure that everyone understood their role in bringing the vision to life and remained motivated and aligned towards its achievement.

Gathering the Team

In the bright and spacious conference room adorned with the company's values, Alex gathered the entire InovaTech team. Today's focus: communicating the company's vision effectively.

"Good morning, everyone," Alex greeted, his voice resonating with warmth and enthusiasm. "Today, we have an important task ahead of us. We need to ensure that every member of our team understands and embraces our vision, as it will guide our journey forward."

Clarifying the Vision

Alex began by reiterating the company's vision, projecting it onto a large screen for all to see. He explained each aspect of the vision in detail, emphasizing its significance and relevance to the team's work.

"Our vision is not just a statement—it's a shared commitment to creating a better future through innovation," Alex declared. "It's what drives us, inspires us, and guides our decisions every day."

Empowering Every Employee

Next, Alex emphasized the importance of empowering every employee to contribute to the realization of the vision.

"Our vision is not limited to the leadership team," Alex emphasized. "Each and every one of you plays a crucial role in bringing it to life. Your ideas, your passion, and your dedication are what will drive our success."

Communicating with Clarity

To ensure that the vision was effectively communicated throughout the organization, Alex introduced a communication strategy.

"We need to communicate our vision with clarity and consistency," Alex explained. "From company-wide meetings to departmental updates, every communication should reinforce our vision and its importance."

Sharing Success Stories

To illustrate the impact of the vision in action, Alex shared success stories of employees who had exemplified the company's values and contributed to its vision.

"These stories are a testament to the power of our vision," Alex remarked. "They show how each of us can make a difference and bring our vision to life through our everyday actions."

Encouraging Feedback and Collaboration

Alex concluded by encouraging open communication and collaboration among team members.

"Our vision is a living, breathing entity that evolves with our company," Alex stated. "I encourage each of you to share your thoughts, ideas, and feedback as we work together to realize our vision."

Conclusion

As the meeting came to a close, the room was filled with a sense of unity and purpose. Every member of the InovaTech team left the conference room with a renewed understanding of the company's vision and a sense of empowerment to contribute to its achievement.

Alex remained behind, reflecting on the productive meeting. With effective communication and a shared commitment to the vision, he was confident that InovaTech was well-positioned to realize its ambitious goals and lead the industry into a future filled with innovation and success.

Measuring Success: Metrics and KPIs

With the vision communicated effectively, Alex Carter knew that it was essential to establish clear metrics and key performance indicators (KPIs) to measure the progress and success of InovaTech's initiatives. Tracking these metrics would provide valuable insights into the company's performance and ensure alignment with its strategic objectives.

Setting the Stage

In the sleek and modern analytics room, Alex convened the leadership team once again, this time with a focus on establishing metrics and KPIs to measure success.

"Good afternoon, everyone," Alex greeted, his tone focused and determined. "Today, we're diving into the critical task of measuring success. By establishing clear metrics and KPIs, we can track our progress towards achieving our vision and strategic goals."

Defining Metrics and KPIs

Alex began by explaining the difference between metrics and KPIs and their importance in guiding decision-making and evaluating performance.

"Metrics are quantitative measures of performance, while KPIs are specific metrics that are tied to our strategic objectives," Alex clarified. "Together, they provide a comprehensive view of our progress and highlight areas for improvement."

Aligning with Strategic Objectives

Next, Alex led the team through a discussion on how to align metrics and KPIs with InovaTech's strategic objectives.

"Our metrics and KPIs should reflect the key areas of focus outlined in our strategic plan," Alex emphasized. "They should be SMART—specific, measurable, achievable, relevant, and time-bound—to ensure clarity and accountability."

Identifying Key Metrics

The team split into smaller groups, each tasked with identifying key metrics and KPIs for a specific area of focus, such as product development, marketing, or customer satisfaction.

After intense brainstorming and analysis, the groups reconvened to present their proposed metrics and KPIs.

Product Development Metrics

One group focused on product development, proposing metrics such as time to market, product quality, and customer satisfaction ratings as KPIs to measure success in delivering innovative solutions that meet customer needs.

Marketing Metrics

Another group addressed marketing, recommending metrics such as brand awareness, lead generation, and conversion rates as KPIs to evaluate the effectiveness of marketing campaigns and initiatives.

Customer Satisfaction Metrics

The third group highlighted customer satisfaction, proposing metrics such as Net Promoter Score (NPS), customer retention rate, and customer lifetime value as KPIs to assess customer loyalty and satisfaction.

Integrating Metrics and KPIs

As the presentations concluded, Alex synthesized the proposed metrics and KPIs into a cohesive framework, ensuring alignment with InovaTech's strategic objectives.

"These metrics and KPIs provide a comprehensive view of our performance and progress towards achieving our vision," Alex remarked. "By tracking these indicators, we can identify areas of strength and opportunities for improvement, enabling us to make data-driven decisions and drive continuous improvement."

Conclusion

As the meeting adjourned, the leadership team left the analytics room with a clear understanding of the importance of metrics and KPIs in measuring success. Armed with a comprehensive framework for tracking performance, they were ready to drive InovaTech towards its visionary future with confidence and clarity.

Alex remained behind, reviewing the proposed metrics and KPIs with satisfaction. With a robust measurement framework in place, he knew that InovaTech was well-equipped to monitor its progress and achieve its ambitious goals, one milestone at a time.

3

Chapter 3: Building a Culture of Innovation

Encouraging a Growth Mindset

In the heart of InovaTech's headquarters, Alex Carter stood before the assembled team, ready to delve into the crucial task of building a culture of innovation. At the core of this endeavor was the need to encourage a growth mindset—a fundamental belief in the power of learning, resilience, and adaptability to drive innovation and growth.

Setting the Stage

"Good morning, everyone," Alex greeted, his voice resonating with warmth and determination. "Today, we embark on a journey to foster a culture of innovation—a culture where creativity flourishes, ideas are valued, and every member of our team is empowered to make a difference."

Defining the Growth Mindset

Alex began by defining the concept of a growth mindset—a belief that intelligence and abilities can be developed through dedication and hard work.

"A growth mindset is essential for innovation," Alex explained. "It encourages us to embrace challenges, persist in the face of setbacks, and see failure as an opportunity for growth."

Cultivating a Growth Mindset

To cultivate a growth mindset within InovaTech, Alex emphasized the importance of leadership support, continuous learning, and a safe environment for experimentation and risk-taking.

"We, as leaders, must model a growth mindset in our words and actions," Alex asserted. "We need to encourage our teams to stretch beyond their comfort zones, take calculated risks, and learn from both success and failure."

Embracing Challenges

Next, Alex encouraged the team to embrace challenges as opportunities for growth and innovation.

"Challenges are not obstacles—they are invitations to innovate," Alex declared. "When faced with a challenge, approach it with curiosity and determination. Seek out new perspectives, experiment with different approaches, and never underestimate the power of perseverance."

Learning from Failure

Alex shared personal anecdotes of failure and resilience, highlighting the valuable lessons learned from setbacks and mistakes.

"Failure is not the end—it's a stepping stone to success," Alex emphasized. "When we embrace failure as a natural part of the innovation process, we unlock our potential to learn, adapt, and grow stronger."

Celebrating Growth and Progress

To reinforce the importance of a growth mindset, Alex encouraged the team to celebrate growth and progress, no matter how small.

"Every step forward is a victory worth celebrating," Alex affirmed. "By recognizing and acknowledging our progress, we cultivate a culture of positivity, resilience, and continuous improvement."

Conclusion

As the meeting came to a close, the room was filled with a sense of excitement and possibility. The team left the room with a renewed commitment to fostering a growth mindset within InovaTech, knowing that it was the key to unlocking their collective potential for innovation and success.

Alex remained behind, reflecting on the importance of encouraging a growth mindset in driving innovation and growth. With the seeds of a growth mindset planted within InovaTech, he knew that the company was well on its way to building a culture of innovation that would propel them towards a future filled with endless possibilities.

Fostering Open Communication and Collaboration

In the heart of InovaTech's headquarters, Alex Carter stood before the assembled team, ready to continue the journey of building a culture of innovation. Today's focus: fostering open communication and collaboration—a cornerstone of innovation that would enable the team to share ideas, collaborate effectively, and bring their collective vision to life.

Setting the Stage

"Good morning, everyone," Alex greeted, his voice filled with energy and enthusiasm. "Today, we continue our exploration of building a culture of innovation by focusing on the importance of open communication and collaboration. These are the bedrocks upon which great ideas are born and nurtured."

Breaking Down Silos

Alex began by addressing the need to break down silos and encourage cross-departmental communication and collaboration.

"Silos stifle innovation," Alex declared. "To truly innovate, we must break down these barriers and create a culture where ideas flow freely across departments and teams."

Creating a Safe Space for Ideas

Next, Alex emphasized the importance of creating a safe space where team members felt comfortable sharing their ideas, no matter how unconventional or risky they may seem.

"Innovation thrives in an environment where every voice is heard and valued," Alex asserted. "We need to foster a culture where team members feel empowered to speak up, share their ideas, and contribute to the collective vision."

Embracing Diversity of Thought

Alex encouraged the team to embrace diversity of thought and perspective, recognizing that innovation often arises from the collision of different ideas and viewpoints.

"Our differences are our greatest strength," Alex affirmed. "By embracing diversity of thought, we can uncover new insights, challenge assumptions, and push the boundaries of what is possible."

Encouraging Collaboration

To foster collaboration, Alex introduced new initiatives such as cross-functional workshops, brainstorming sessions, and collaborative projects that would bring team members together to solve problems and explore new ideas.

"Collaboration fuels innovation," Alex stated. "By working together, we can leverage our collective expertise and creativity to tackle challenges and drive meaningful change."

Leading by Example

Finally, Alex emphasized the importance of leadership in fostering open communication and collaboration.

"As leaders, it is our responsibility to lead by example," Alex declared. "We must actively listen to our team members, encourage open dialogue, and champion collaboration at every opportunity."

Conclusion

As the meeting came to a close, the room buzzed with excitement and anticipation. The team left the room inspired and motivated, ready to embrace open communication and collaboration as they continued their journey of innovation at InovaTech.

Alex remained behind, filled with a sense of pride and optimism. With a culture of open communication and collaboration taking root within InovaTech, he knew that the company was well on its way to unlocking its full potential and achieving greatness in the ever-evolving world of technology.

Rewarding Creativity and Risk-Taking

In the vibrant atmosphere of InovaTech's headquarters, Alex Carter stood before the assembled team, ready to delve into the critical aspect of building a culture of innovation: rewarding creativity and risk-taking. Alex knew that recognizing and incentivizing innovation would not only motivate the team but also reinforce the values of experimentation and boldness essential for driving innovation forward.

Setting the Stage

"Good afternoon, everyone," Alex greeted, his voice brimming with enthusiasm. "Today, we explore the importance of rewarding creativity and risk-taking—a key pillar in our journey to foster a culture of innovation. It's not enough to encourage bold ideas; we must also celebrate and reward them."

Valuing Creative Contributions

Alex began by emphasizing the importance of valuing and recognizing creative contributions from every member of the team, regardless of their role or seniority.

"Creativity knows no hierarchy," Alex declared. "We must cultivate an environment where every idea is valued and every contribution is celebrated. By doing so, we unlock the full potential of our team and unleash a wave of innovation."

Recognizing Courageous Innovation

Next, Alex turned his attention to the importance of recognizing and rewarding risk-taking—the willingness to pursue bold ideas and embrace uncertainty.

"Innovation requires courage," Alex affirmed. "We must recognize and celebrate those who dare to challenge the status quo, take calculated risks, and push the boundaries of what is possible. It's through their courage that we pave the way for breakthrough innovation."

Implementing Reward Mechanisms

To incentivize creativity and risk-taking, Alex introduced new reward mechanisms such as innovation awards, recognition programs, and incentive bonuses for successful innovation initiatives.

"Rewards send a powerful message," Alex explained. "They signal to our team that we value and appreciate their creative efforts, and they motivate others to follow suit. By rewarding innovation, we create a culture where bold ideas are not only encouraged but also celebrated."

Showcasing Success Stories

To inspire the team and reinforce the importance of creativity and risk-taking, Alex shared success stories of innovative projects and initiatives that had made a significant impact on the company.

"These success stories are a testament to the power of creativity and risk-taking," Alex remarked. "They remind us that innovation is not just a buzzword—it's a mindset, a way of thinking and working that drives us forward."

Empowering Every Team Member

Finally, Alex encouraged every team member to embrace their role as innovators and change-makers, regardless of their title or department.

"Innovation is not the sole responsibility of a select few," Alex asserted. "It's a collective effort that requires the participation and commitment of every member of our team. Together, we can achieve greatness and redefine the future of technology."

Conclusion

As the meeting came to a close, the room buzzed with excitement and anticipation. The team left the room inspired and motivated, ready to unleash their creativity and embrace risk-taking as they continued their journey of innovation at InovaTech.

Alex remained behind, filled with a sense of pride and optimism. With a culture of rewarding creativity and risk-taking taking root within InovaTech, he knew that the company was well on its way to achieving its bold vision and making a lasting impact on the world.

Breaking Down Silos: Promoting Cross-Functional Teams

In the dynamic environment of InovaTech's headquarters, Alex Carter stood before the assembled team, ready to explore the transformative power of breaking down silos and promoting cross-functional teams. Alex understood that fostering collaboration across departments would not only facilitate knowledge sharing but also spur creativity and innovation by bringing diverse perspectives together.

Setting the Stage

"Good morning, everyone," Alex greeted, his voice resonating with energy and purpose. "Today, we embark on a journey to break down silos and promote cross-functional teams—

a critical step in our quest to foster a culture of innovation. By working together across departments, we can unlock new insights, drive innovation, and achieve our shared goals."

Recognizing the Impact of Silos

Alex began by addressing the negative impact of silos on innovation, productivity, and collaboration within the organization.

"Silos create barriers," Alex explained. "They hinder communication, stifle creativity, and impede progress. To truly innovate, we must break down these barriers and create a culture where collaboration flourishes and ideas flow freely."

Promoting Cross-Functional Collaboration

Next, Alex emphasized the importance of promoting cross-functional collaboration—bringing together individuals from different departments and disciplines to work towards common goals.

"Cross-functional collaboration is a catalyst for innovation," Alex asserted. "By bringing together diverse perspectives, skills, and experiences, we can tackle complex challenges, generate creative solutions, and drive meaningful change."

Creating Opportunities for Collaboration

To promote cross-functional collaboration, Alex introduced new initiatives such as cross-departmental projects, task forces, and workshops that would bring team members from different departments together to collaborate on specific initiatives.

"These opportunities for collaboration are not just about working together on projects," Alex explained. "They're about building relationships, sharing knowledge, and learning from one another. By breaking down silos, we can unleash the full potential of our team and achieve extraordinary results."

Breaking Down Barriers

Alex encouraged team members to actively seek out opportunities for cross-functional collaboration and break down any remaining barriers that may exist between departments.

"Breaking down silos requires effort from each and every one of us," Alex stated. "We must be proactive in reaching out to colleagues from other departments, seeking their input, and collaborating on projects that span across disciplines. Together, we can overcome any obstacles and achieve greatness."

Celebrating Collaborative Success

Finally, Alex emphasized the importance of celebrating the success of cross-functional collaboration and recognizing the contributions of individuals and teams who work together to achieve shared goals.

"When we celebrate collaborative success, we reinforce the importance of cross-functional collaboration and inspire others to follow suit," Alex concluded. "Together, we can break down silos, promote collaboration, and build a culture of innovation that propels us towards our vision of a better future."

Conclusion

As the meeting came to a close, the room was filled with a sense of unity and purpose. The team left the room inspired and motivated, ready to embrace cross-functional collaboration as they continued their journey of innovation at InovaTech.

Alex remained behind, filled with a sense of pride and optimism. With a culture of collaboration taking root within InovaTech, he knew that the company was well on its way to achieving its ambitious goals and making a lasting impact on the world.

Creating a Safe Space for Experimentation

In the vibrant atmosphere of InovaTech's headquarters, Alex Carter stood before the assembled team, ready to explore the importance of creating a safe space for experimentation—a crucial element in fostering a culture of innovation. Alex knew that encouraging team members to take risks and explore new ideas without fear of failure would unlock their creativity and drive transformative innovation.

Setting the Stage

"Good afternoon, everyone," Alex greeted, his voice filled with warmth and encouragement. "Today, we dive into the critical aspect of creating a safe space for experimentation—a key ingredient in our recipe for fostering innovation. By providing our team with the freedom to explore, take risks, and learn from failure, we unlock their full creative potential and drive meaningful change."

Embracing a Culture of Experimentation

Alex began by emphasizing the importance of embracing a culture of experimentation—one where curiosity is encouraged, and failure is seen as an opportunity for growth.

"Innovation is born from experimentation," Alex declared. "We must create an environment where team members feel empowered to try new things, take calculated risks, and learn from both success and failure. It's through experimentation that we discover new ideas, refine existing processes, and push the boundaries of what is possible."

Encouraging Risk-Taking

Next, Alex encouraged team members to embrace risk-taking as a necessary component of the innovation process.

"Risk-taking is not reckless—it's essential," Alex asserted. "We must encourage our team members to step outside their comfort zones, challenge the status quo, and pursue bold ideas that have the potential to drive significant change. It's through taking risks that we achieve breakthrough innovation and create a better future for our company and our customers."

Providing Support and Resources

To facilitate experimentation, Alex committed to providing team members with the support and resources they needed to explore new ideas and initiatives.

"We must equip our team with the tools, resources, and support they need to experiment effectively," Alex stated. "Whether it's access to funding, time for exploration, or mentorship from experienced innovators, we must invest in our team's success and create an environment where experimentation thrives."

Learning from Failure

Alex emphasized the importance of learning from failure and using it as a catalyst for growth and improvement.

"Failure is not the end—it's the beginning of something new," Alex affirmed. "We must encourage our team members to embrace failure as a natural part of the innovation process, to learn from their mistakes, and to use those lessons to iterate and improve. It's through failure that we gain valuable insights, build resilience, and ultimately achieve success."

Celebrating Experimentation

Finally, Alex emphasized the importance of celebrating experimentation and recognizing the efforts of team members who take risks and pursue innovative ideas.

"When we celebrate experimentation, we reinforce its importance and inspire others to follow suit," Alex concluded. "By creating a culture where experimentation is celebrated and supported, we create an environment where innovation flourishes, and our team members can reach their full potential."

Conclusion

As the meeting came to a close, the room was filled with a sense of excitement and possibility. The team left the room inspired and motivated, ready to embrace experimentation as they continued their journey of innovation at InovaTech.

Alex remained behind, filled with a sense of pride and optimism. With a culture of experimentation taking root within InovaTech, he knew that the company was well on its way to achieving its ambitious goals and making a lasting impact on the world.

4

Chapter 4: Leading Through Change

Understanding the Change Curve

In the boardroom of InovaTech's headquarters, Alex Carter stood before the leadership team, ready to delve into the complexities of leading through change. Today's focus: understanding the change curve—a crucial concept that would guide the team through the inevitable challenges and transitions that lay ahead.

Setting the Stage

"Good morning, everyone," Alex greeted, his voice steady and reassuring. "Today, we embark on a journey to navigate the complexities of change—a journey that requires understanding the change curve and its implications for our organization. By embracing change and guiding our team through its various stages, we can emerge stronger and more resilient than ever before."

Introducing the Change Curve

Alex began by introducing the concept of the change curve—a model that describes the psychological stages individuals experience when confronted with change.

"The change curve is a roadmap for navigating change," Alex explained. "It helps us understand the emotional journey our team members will undergo as we navigate through periods of uncertainty and transition."

Denial and Resistance

Alex highlighted the first stage of the change curve: denial and resistance—a natural reaction to the shock of change.

"In this stage, team members may resist change, clinging to familiar routines and processes," Alex noted. "It's essential to acknowledge these feelings and provide support and reassurance as we navigate through this initial phase."

Anger and Frustration

Next, Alex discussed the second stage of the change curve: anger and frustration—a period marked by feelings of resentment and disillusionment.

"In this stage, team members may express frustration and anger as they come to terms with the reality of change," Alex observed. "It's important to listen to their concerns, validate their emotions, and provide clear communication to address any misconceptions or fears."

Exploration and Acceptance

Alex then turned to the third stage of the change curve: exploration and acceptance—a phase characterized by curiosity and openness to new possibilities.

"In this stage, team members begin to explore the potential benefits of change and embrace new ways of thinking and working," Alex remarked. "It's crucial to foster a sense of curiosity and encourage experimentation as we navigate through this transitional period."

Commitment and Integration

Finally, Alex discussed the fourth stage of the change curve: commitment and integration—a phase where team members fully embrace change and integrate it into their daily routines and practices.

"In this stage, team members demonstrate a high level of commitment to change and actively contribute to its success," Alex observed. "It's essential to celebrate achievements, recognize progress, and reinforce the positive impact of change as we move forward."

Leading Through Change

As the meeting came to a close, Alex reiterated the importance of understanding the change curve and guiding the team through its various stages with empathy, resilience, and determination.

"Change is inevitable," Alex concluded. "But by understanding the change curve and leading with compassion and clarity, we can navigate through periods of uncertainty and emerge stronger and more united than ever before."

Conclusion

The leadership team left the boardroom with a renewed understanding of the change curve and its implications for leading through change. Armed with this knowledge, they were ready to guide InovaTech through the challenges and transitions that lay ahead, confident in their ability to navigate change and emerge stronger on the other side.

The Psychology of Change: Managing Resistance

In the tranquil ambiance of InovaTech's conference room, Alex Carter stood before the leadership team, poised to explore the intricacies of managing resistance—a critical aspect of leading through change. Today's focus: delving into the psychology of change and understanding how to navigate resistance effectively.

Setting the Stage

"Good afternoon, everyone," Alex greeted, his tone empathetic yet resolute. "Today, we delve into the complex terrain of managing resistance—a challenge inherent in leading through change. By understanding the psychology behind resistance and implementing strategies to address it, we can foster a culture of resilience and adaptability within our organization."

Unpacking Resistance

Alex began by unpacking the concept of resistance, explaining its underlying psychological drivers and manifestations.

"Resistance is a natural response to change," Alex explained. "It stems from fear of the unknown, loss of control, and discomfort with uncertainty. As leaders, it's essential to recognize and acknowledge these feelings, as they can significantly impact our team's ability to adapt and embrace change."

Empathizing with Emotions

Alex emphasized the importance of empathizing with the emotions underlying resistance, acknowledging that change can evoke a range of feelings, including fear, anxiety, and frustration.

"We must recognize that resistance is not a sign of weakness—it's a natural reaction to change," Alex noted. "By empathizing with our team members' emotions and validating their concerns, we can create a safe space for dialogue and foster a sense of trust and understanding."

Communicating with Clarity

To address resistance effectively, Alex stressed the importance of clear and transparent communication, providing context, rationale, and guidance throughout the change process.

"Communication is key," Alex affirmed. "We must communicate early and often, sharing the 'why' behind change, outlining its potential benefits, and addressing any misconceptions or fears. By keeping our team informed and engaged, we can

Involving Stakeholders

Alex highlighted the importance of involving stakeholders in the change process, soliciting their input, and empowering them to contribute to decision-making and problem-solving.

"Change is a collective effort," Alex stated. "We must involve our team members in the change process, soliciting their feedback, addressing their concerns, and empowering them to be active participants in shaping the future of our organization. By involving stakeholders, we foster ownership and commitment to change."

Providing Support and Resources

To help team members navigate through resistance, Alex committed to providing support and resources, including training, coaching, and counseling.

"We must support our team members through the change process," Alex affirmed. "Whether it's providing training to develop new skills, offering coaching to navigate challenges, or offering counseling to address emotional concerns, we must equip our team with the support and resources they need to adapt and thrive."

Celebrating Progress

Finally, Alex emphasized the importance of celebrating progress and recognizing the efforts of team members who demonstrate resilience and adaptability in the face of change.

"Change is a journey," Alex concluded. "By celebrating small wins, recognizing achievements, and acknowledging the efforts of our team, we reinforce the positive impact of change and inspire others to embrace it wholeheartedly."

Conclusion

As the meeting came to a close, the leadership team left the conference room with a renewed understanding of the psychology of change and strategies for managing resistance effectively. Armed with empathy, clarity, and support, they were ready to lead InovaTech through the challenges and opportunities that lay ahead, confident in their ability to navigate change and emerge stronger on the other side.

Developing Change Management Strategies

In the tranquil ambiance of InovaTech's conference room, Alex Carter stood before the leadership team, ready to delve into the intricacies of developing change management strategies—a pivotal aspect of leading through change. Today's focus: crafting effective approaches to guide the organization through periods of transition and transformation.

Setting the Stage

"Good afternoon, everyone," Alex greeted, his voice projecting confidence and determination. "Today, we embark on the essential task of developing change management strategies—a roadmap that will guide us through the complexities of change and ensure our organization emerges stronger and more resilient than ever before."

Acknowledging the Need for Change

Alex began by acknowledging the need for change and the importance of proactively managing it to achieve desired outcomes.

"Change is inevitable," Alex stated. "But how we navigate change determines our success. By developing clear and effective change management strategies, we can minimize disruption, maximize engagement, and achieve our organizational goals."

Assessing the Impact of Change

Next, Alex emphasized the importance of assessing the impact of change on various stakeholders, including employees, customers, and partners.

"We must understand how change will affect our stakeholders," Alex noted. "By conducting thorough assessments and engaging with stakeholders, we can identify potential challenges, anticipate resistance, and develop strategies to address them proactively."

Communicating the Vision

Alex stressed the importance of clear and consistent communication in change management, ensuring that everyone understands the vision, rationale, and benefits of change.

"Communication is the cornerstone of change management," Alex affirmed. "We must articulate the 'why' behind change, outline its objectives and benefits, and provide regular updates and feedback channels to keep stakeholders informed and engaged."

Empowering and Involving Employees

To foster ownership and commitment to change, Alex emphasized the importance of empowering and involving employees in the change process.

"Our employees are our greatest asset," Alex declared. "We must involve them in decision-making, solicit their input and feedback, and empower them to be champions of change within their teams. By fostering a sense of ownership and involvement, we can build momentum and drive successful change."

Providing Support and Resources

Alex committed to providing support and resources to help employees navigate through change, including training, coaching, and emotional support.

"We must support our employees through every stage of change," Alex stated. "Whether it's providing training to develop new skills, offering coaching to navigate challenges, or offering emotional support to address concerns, we must equip our employees with the tools and resources they need to succeed."

Monitoring and Adjusting

Finally, Alex emphasized the importance of monitoring progress and adjusting strategies as needed to ensure successful implementation of change.

"Change is dynamic," Alex concluded. "We must continuously monitor progress, solicit feedback, and adjust our strategies as needed to address emerging challenges and opportunities. By remaining agile and adaptable, we can navigate change effectively and achieve our desired outcomes."

Conclusion

As the meeting came to a close, the leadership team left the conference room with a clear understanding of the importance of developing change management strategies and a commitment to proactively guiding InovaTech through periods of change and transformation. Armed with clarity, empathy, and determination, they were ready to lead their organization towards a future filled with innovation and success.

Engaging Stakeholders in the Change Process

In the boardroom of InovaTech's headquarters, Alex Carter stood before the leadership team, prepared to explore the vital aspect of engaging stakeholders in the change process. Today's focus: fostering collaboration and participation from all levels of the organization to ensure successful implementation of change initiatives.

Setting the Stage

"Good morning, everyone," Alex greeted, his voice resonating with energy and purpose. "Today, we dive into the critical task of engaging stakeholders in the change process—a journey that requires collaboration, communication, and commitment from every member of our organization. By involving stakeholders in decision-making and implementation, we can harness the collective wisdom and expertise of our team to drive meaningful change."

Acknowledging Stakeholder Perspectives

Alex began by acknowledging the importance of understanding and addressing the perspectives and concerns of stakeholders impacted by change.

"Our stakeholders are the heart of our organization," Alex stated. "We must listen to their voices, understand their perspectives, and address their concerns with empathy and respect. By acknowledging their contributions and involving them in the change process, we can build trust and collaboration."

Communicating with Transparency

Next, Alex emphasized the importance of transparent communication in engaging stakeholders, ensuring that they are informed and empowered to participate in the change process.

"Transparency builds trust," Alex affirmed. "We must communicate openly and honestly with our stakeholders, sharing information about the reasons for change, its objectives, and the expected impact. By providing clear and consistent communication, we create a foundation for collaboration and engagement."

Involving Stakeholders in Decision-Making

To foster ownership and commitment to change, Alex stressed the importance of involving stakeholders in decision-making and problem-solving.

"Our stakeholders have valuable insights and perspectives," Alex noted. "We must involve them in decision-making processes, solicit their input and feedback, and empower them to contribute to the development and implementation of change initiatives. By fostering a sense of ownership and involvement, we can drive meaningful and sustainable change."

Providing Opportunities for Input

Alex committed to providing opportunities for stakeholders to provide input and feedback throughout the change process, ensuring that their voices are heard and valued.

"We must create channels for stakeholders to share their ideas, concerns, and feedback," Alex stated. "Whether it's through town hall meetings, focus groups, or online forums, we must provide opportunities for stakeholders to participate in the change process and contribute to its success."

Recognizing and Celebrating Contributions

Finally, Alex emphasized the importance of recognizing and celebrating the contributions of stakeholders to the change process, reinforcing their sense of value and commitment.

"We must celebrate the achievements and milestones of our stakeholders," Alex concluded. "By recognizing their contributions and celebrating their successes, we show our appreciation and reinforce their commitment to change. Together, we can achieve our shared goals and create a brighter future for our organization."

Conclusion

As the meeting came to a close, the leadership team left the boardroom with a renewed commitment to engaging stakeholders in the change process. Armed with empathy, transparency, and collaboration, they were ready to harness the collective wisdom and expertise of their team to drive meaningful change and achieve their organizational goals.

Leading by Example: Modeling Adaptive Behavior

In the serene ambiance of InovaTech's executive suite, Alex Carter stood before the leadership team, ready to explore the transformative power of leading by example during times of change. Today's focus: modeling adaptive behavior and demonstrating the resilience and agility needed to navigate through periods of uncertainty and transformation.

Setting the Stage

"Good afternoon, everyone," Alex greeted, his voice imbued with conviction and determination. "Today, we delve into the critical role of leading by example—a cornerstone of effective leadership, especially during times of change. By modeling adaptive behavior and demonstrating resilience in the face of uncertainty, we can inspire our team to embrace change and navigate through challenges with confidence and determination."

Embracing Adaptability

Alex began by emphasizing the importance of adaptability in leadership, highlighting the need for leaders to be flexible, open-minded, and willing to embrace change.

"As leaders, we must be adaptable," Alex stated. "We must be willing to step outside our comfort zones, embrace new ideas and perspectives, and adjust our approaches as needed to navigate through uncertainty and change."

Demonstrating Resilience

Next, Alex stressed the importance of resilience in leadership, acknowledging that setbacks and challenges are inevitable during times of change.

"Resilience is key," Alex affirmed. "We must demonstrate perseverance, optimism, and resilience in the face of adversity, showing our team that setbacks are not roadblocks but opportunities for growth and learning."

Communicating with Clarity and Confidence

Alex emphasized the importance of clear and confident communication in inspiring confidence and trust during times of change.

"Communication is essential," Alex noted. "We must communicate with clarity and confidence, providing a clear vision, direction, and purpose to guide our team through change. By instilling confidence and trust in our team, we can inspire them to follow our lead and embrace change with conviction."

Remaining Calm Under Pressure

To inspire calm and stability during times of uncertainty, Alex committed to remaining composed and level-headed in the face of challenges.

"We must remain calm under pressure," Alex stated. "Our team looks to us for guidance and reassurance during times of change. By remaining composed and level-headed, we can inspire confidence and stability, even in the midst of uncertainty."

Adapting to Feedback and Challenges

Alex emphasized the importance of being receptive to feedback and willing to adapt to changing circumstances and challenges.

"We must be open to feedback," Alex affirmed. "We must listen to the concerns and ideas of our team members, adapt our approaches as needed, and demonstrate a willingness to learn and grow. By modeling adaptive behavior, we create a culture of continuous improvement and resilience within our organization."

Conclusion

As the meeting came to a close, the leadership team left the executive suite with a renewed commitment to leading by example during times of change. Armed with adaptability, resilience, and confidence, they were ready to inspire their team to embrace change, navigate through challenges, and emerge stronger and more united than ever before.

Sustaining Momentum: Ensuring Long-Term Change

In the tranquil atmosphere of InovaTech's conference room, Alex Carter stood before the leadership team, poised to explore the crucial aspect of sustaining momentum—a vital component of leading through change. Today's focus: ensuring that change initiatives result in long-term transformation and lasting impact.

Setting the Stage

"Good morning, everyone," Alex greeted, his voice brimming with determination and resolve. "Today, we delve into the essential task of sustaining momentum—a journey that requires dedication, perseverance, and foresight. By implementing strategies to ensure long-term change, we can solidify our organization's position as a leader in innovation and drive continued success in the ever-evolving landscape of technology."

Reinforcing the Vision

Alex began by reinforcing the organization's vision and purpose, reminding the team of the long-term goals and objectives driving their change initiatives.

"Our vision is our compass," Alex affirmed. "We must remain steadfast in our commitment to our vision, ensuring that every change initiative aligns with our long-term goals and contributes to our overarching mission."

Embedding Change into Culture

Next, Alex emphasized the importance of embedding change into the organization's culture, making it a part of its DNA and identity.

"Change must become our culture," Alex declared. "We must institutionalize change by integrating it into our processes, systems, and behaviors. By embedding change into our culture, we create a foundation for sustained success and continuous improvement."

Empowering Change Agents

Alex stressed the importance of empowering change agents throughout the organization, providing them with the resources, authority, and support needed to drive change initiatives forward.

"Our change agents are our catalysts for transformation," Alex noted. "We must empower them to lead change initiatives, provide them with the necessary resources and support, and celebrate their achievements. By empowering change agents, we ensure that change becomes ingrained in our organization's DNA."

Monitoring Progress and Adjusting Strategies

To sustain momentum, Alex committed to monitoring progress and adjusting strategies as needed to address emerging challenges and opportunities.

"We must remain vigilant," Alex stated. "We must continuously monitor progress, solicit feedback, and adjust our strategies as needed to ensure that change initiatives remain on track and aligned with our long-term goals."

Celebrating Milestones and Successes

Alex emphasized the importance of celebrating milestones and successes along the change journey, recognizing the efforts of individuals and teams who contribute to long-term transformation.

"We must celebrate our successes," Alex affirmed. "By recognizing and celebrating milestones along the change journey, we reinforce the importance of change, inspire our team, and create momentum for continued progress."

Fostering a Culture of Continuous Improvement

Finally, Alex stressed the importance of fostering a culture of continuous improvement, encouraging the team to embrace change as a catalyst for growth and innovation.

"Change is not a destination—it's a journey," Alex concluded. "We must embrace change as a constant in our organization, continually striving for improvement and innovation. By fostering a culture of continuous improvement, we ensure that our organization remains adaptable, resilient, and successful in the face of change."

Conclusion

As the meeting came to a close, the leadership team left the conference room with a renewed commitment to sustaining momentum and driving long-term change within InovaTech. Armed with vision, empowerment, and resilience, they were ready to lead their organization into the future, confident in their ability to navigate change and achieve lasting success.

5

Chapter 5: Leveraging Technology and Innovation

The Role of Technology in Modern Leadership

In the state-of-the-art innovation hub of InovaTech, Alex Carter stood before the leadership team, ready to explore the transformative role of technology in modern leadership. Today's focus: understanding how technology can empower leaders to drive innovation, enhance productivity, and unlock new opportunities in a rapidly evolving digital landscape.

Setting the Stage

"Good afternoon, everyone," Alex greeted, his voice infused with excitement and anticipation. "Today, we embark on a journey to explore the dynamic intersection of technology and leadership—a realm where innovation knows no bounds, and possibilities are endless. By harnessing the power of technology, we can redefine what it means to lead in the digital age and unlock new opportunities for growth and success."

Embracing Digital Transformation

Alex began by emphasizing the importance of embracing digital transformation as a fundamental aspect of modern leadership.

"Digital transformation is reshaping the business landscape," Alex stated. "As leaders, we must embrace technology as a catalyst for change, leveraging its power to drive innovation, streamline processes, and create value for our customers and stakeholders."

Enhancing Decision-Making with Data

Next, Alex highlighted the transformative impact of data-driven decision-making on leadership effectiveness.

"Data is our most valuable asset," Alex affirmed. "By harnessing the power of data analytics and insights, we can make informed decisions, identify trends and patterns, and drive strategic initiatives with precision and confidence."

Empowering Collaboration and Communication

Alex emphasized the importance of leveraging technology to foster collaboration and communication within and across teams.

"Technology has the power to connect us like never before," Alex noted. "We must embrace digital tools and platforms that facilitate collaboration, communication, and knowledge sharing, enabling our teams to work together seamlessly and achieve our shared goals."

Driving Innovation with Emerging Technologies

To drive innovation, Alex committed to exploring and leveraging emerging technologies that have the potential to disrupt industries and create new opportunities.

"Innovation is our North Star," Alex declared. "We must stay ahead of the curve by exploring emerging technologies such as artificial intelligence, machine learning, and blockchain, and identifying opportunities to leverage them to create value for our organization and customers."

Navigating Ethical and Social Implications

Alex acknowledged the importance of navigating the ethical and social implications of technology in leadership, emphasizing the need for responsible and ethical use of technology to mitigate risks and ensure positive impact.

"Technology is a double-edged sword," Alex cautioned. "As leaders, we must be mindful of its ethical and social implications, ensuring that our use of technology is aligned with our values and principles and contributes to the greater good."

Conclusion

As the meeting came to a close, the leadership team left the innovation hub with a renewed appreciation for the transformative role of technology in modern leadership. Armed with vision, innovation, and ethical responsibility, they were ready to harness the power of technology to drive positive change and lead InovaTech into a future filled with endless possibilities.

Emerging Technologies: Opportunities and Challenges

In the futuristic confines of InovaTech's research and development lab, Alex Carter stood before the leadership team, poised to explore the thrilling realm of emerging technologies. Today's focus: uncovering the boundless opportunities and navigating the complex challenges presented by the rapid evolution of technology.

Setting the Stage

"Good morning, everyone," Alex greeted, his voice alive with anticipation. "Today, we embark on an exhilarating journey into the world of emerging technologies—a landscape where innovation knows no limits, and the possibilities are as vast as the imagination. By embracing these cutting-edge technologies, we can unlock new opportunities for growth and transformation, while also navigating the challenges they present with foresight and resilience."

Embracing the Promise of Innovation

Alex began by emphasizing the transformative potential of emerging technologies, highlighting the promise they hold for revolutionizing industries and reshaping the future.

"Emerging technologies are the engines of innovation," Alex

stated. "From artificial intelligence and quantum computing to biotechnology and augmented reality, these groundbreaking innovations have the power to revolutionize how we live, work, and interact with the world around us."

Seizing Opportunities for Disruption

Next, Alex underscored the importance of seizing opportunities for disruption presented by emerging technologies, encouraging the team to think boldly and embrace experimentation.

"Disruption is our greatest opportunity," Alex affirmed. "We must be bold in our exploration of emerging technologies, seizing opportunities to disrupt industries, create new markets, and drive sustainable growth for our organization."

Navigating Complex Challenges

However, Alex acknowledged that with great opportunity comes great responsibility, and he urged the team to approach the adoption of emerging technologies with caution and foresight.

"Change brings challenges," Alex cautioned. "As we embrace emerging technologies, we must also navigate complex challenges, including ethical considerations, cybersecurity threats, and the potential for job displacement. It's essential that we approach these challenges with foresight and diligence to mitigate risks and ensure positive outcomes."

Fostering Innovation and Collaboration

To overcome these challenges, Alex stressed the importance of fostering a culture of innovation and collaboration within the organization, encouraging interdisciplinary approaches and partnerships with external stakeholders.

"Innovation thrives on collaboration," Alex noted. "We must break down silos within our organization and foster collaboration across disciplines, departments, and industries. By leveraging the collective expertise and creativity of our team and partners, we can overcome challenges and drive meaningful innovation."

Investing in Talent and Skills Development

Alex committed to investing in talent and skills development to ensure that the organization remains at the forefront of emerging technologies.

"Our greatest asset is our people," Alex declared. "We must invest in talent development and skills training to ensure that our team remains equipped with the knowledge and expertise needed to harness the full potential of emerging technologies."

Conclusion

As the meeting drew to a close, the leadership team left the research and development lab with a renewed sense of excitement and determination. Armed with a deep understanding of the opportunities and challenges presented by emerging technologies, they were ready to embrace innovation, navigate complexity, and lead InovaTech into a future shaped by boundless possibilities.

Digital Transformation: Strategies for Leaders

In the sleek confines of InovaTech's digital strategy war room, Alex Carter stood before the leadership team, prepared to delve into the intricacies of digital transformation. Today's focus: unveiling the strategies that leaders can employ to navigate the complexities of digital transformation and drive organizational success in the digital age.

Setting the Stage

"Good afternoon, everyone," Alex greeted, his voice infused with purpose and determination. "Today, we embark on a transformative journey into the realm of digital transformation—a journey that will redefine how we operate, innovate, and deliver value in the digital age. By embracing digital transformation and implementing effective strategies, we can position InovaTech as a leader in the digital landscape and unlock new opportunities for growth and success."

Embracing a Digital Mindset

Alex began by emphasizing the importance of embracing a digital mindset—a fundamental shift in thinking that enables leaders to leverage technology to drive innovation and create value.

"Digital transformation starts with mindset," Alex affirmed. "We must adopt a digital-first mentality, embracing technology as a strategic enabler that empowers us to reimagine our processes, products, and business models."

Empowering Agile Practices

Next, Alex highlighted the importance of empowering agile practices to drive digital transformation initiatives forward with speed and flexibility.

"Agility is our ally," Alex declared. "We must embrace agile methodologies and practices that enable us to respond quickly to changing market dynamics, customer needs, and technological advancements. By fostering a culture of agility, we can accelerate our digital transformation journey and stay ahead of the curve."

Investing in Innovation

Alex stressed the importance of investing in innovation to drive digital transformation, encouraging leaders to allocate resources and support to initiatives that drive meaningful change and create value.

"Innovation is our engine of growth," Alex noted. "We must invest in innovation—whether it's through research and development, partnerships with startups, or internal incubation programs—to drive digital transformation and unlock new opportunities for our organization."

Fostering a Culture of Experimentation

To drive innovation, Alex emphasized the importance of fostering a culture of experimentation within the organization, encouraging leaders to embrace failure as a learning opportunity and empower teams to take calculated risks.

"Experimentation fuels innovation," Alex affirmed. "We must create a safe space for experimentation, where teams are encouraged to test new ideas, iterate quickly, and learn from failure. By fostering a culture of experimentation, we can drive continuous innovation and drive digital transformation forward."

Embracing Customer-Centricity

Finally, Alex underscored the importance of embracing customer-centricity in driving digital transformation, urging leaders to prioritize the needs and preferences of customers in all digital initiatives.

"Our customers are at the heart of everything we do," Alex stated. "We must prioritize customer-centricity in our digital transformation efforts, leveraging technology to deliver personalized experiences, streamline processes, and create value for our customers."

Conclusion

As the meeting came to a close, the leadership team left the digital strategy war room with a renewed sense of purpose and clarity. Armed with strategies for driving digital transformation, they were ready to lead InovaTech into a future defined by innovation, agility, and customer-centricity.

Utilizing Data for Informed Decision-Making

In the sleek conference room of InovaTech's headquarters, Alex Carter stood before the leadership team, prepared to explore the transformative power of data-driven decision-making. Today's focus: uncovering the strategies that leaders can employ to harness the wealth of data available in the digital age and make informed decisions that drive organizational success.

Setting the Stage

"Good morning, everyone," Alex greeted, his voice resonating with confidence and purpose. "Today, we dive into the realm of data-driven decision-making—a critical component of modern leadership that empowers us to leverage the wealth of data available to drive strategic initiatives, enhance performance, and create value for our organization and stakeholders."

Embracing the Data Revolution

Alex began by emphasizing the transformative impact of the data revolution on decision-making processes, highlighting the unprecedented access to data and insights that technology provides.

"The data revolution has democratized information," Alex noted. "We now have access to vast amounts of data—from customer preferences and market trends to operational performance and employee productivity—that can inform our decision-making and drive strategic initiatives forward."

Leveraging Advanced Analytics

Next, Alex underscored the importance of leveraging advanced analytics and data visualization tools to extract actionable insights from data and drive informed decision-making.

"Data is only valuable if we can extract meaningful insights from it," Alex affirmed. "We must invest in advanced analytics capabilities and data visualization tools that enable us to analyze complex data sets, identify patterns and trends, and make informed decisions with confidence and clarity."

Implementing a Data-Driven Culture

To embed data-driven decision-making into the organization's culture, Alex stressed the importance of promoting data literacy and fostering a culture of curiosity and experimentation around data.

"Data-driven decision-making starts with culture," Alex declared. "We must promote data literacy among our team members, providing training and resources to enhance their understanding of data and analytics. By fostering a culture of curiosity and experimentation around data, we empower our team to leverage data to drive innovation and performance."

Prioritizing Data Security and Privacy

Alex acknowledged the importance of prioritizing data security and privacy in data-driven decision-making, emphasizing the need to establish robust policies and practices to protect sensitive information.

"With great data comes great responsibility," Alex cautioned.

"We must prioritize data security and privacy in all aspects of our data-driven decision-making processes, ensuring that sensitive information is protected from unauthorized access or misuse."

Collaborating Across Departments

Finally, Alex emphasized the importance of collaboration across departments and functions to maximize the value of data and drive organizational success.

"Data knows no boundaries," Alex affirmed. "We must break down silos within our organization and promote collaboration across departments and functions to maximize the value of data and drive informed decision-making at every level."

Conclusion

As the meeting drew to a close, the leadership team left the conference room with a renewed appreciation for the power of data-driven decision-making in driving organizational success. Armed with strategies for leveraging data effectively, they were ready to embrace the data revolution and lead InovaTech into a future defined by innovation, agility, and informed decision-making.

Cybersecurity and Ethical Considerations

In the secure confines of InovaTech's cybersecurity center, Alex Carter stood before the leadership team, prepared to navigate the complex landscape of cybersecurity and ethical considerations in the digital age. Today's focus: understanding the importance of safeguarding data and upholding ethical principles in the midst of technological advancement.

Setting the Stage

"Good afternoon, everyone," Alex greeted, his voice tinged with gravity. "Today, we confront a critical aspect of technology and innovation—cybersecurity and ethical considerations. As leaders in the digital age, it's our responsibility to protect the integrity of our data and uphold ethical principles in all our endeavors. By prioritizing cybersecurity and ethical considerations, we can safeguard our organization's reputation and build trust with our stakeholders."

Safeguarding Data Integrity

Alex began by emphasizing the importance of safeguarding data integrity and protecting against cyber threats that could compromise sensitive information.

"Our data is our most valuable asset," Alex affirmed. "We must implement robust cybersecurity measures to protect against unauthorized access, data breaches, and cyberattacks that could jeopardize the integrity and confidentiality of our data."

Upholding Ethical Principles

Next, Alex underscored the importance of upholding ethical principles in all aspects of technology and innovation, emphasizing the need to prioritize integrity, transparency, and accountability in decision-making.

"Ethics must guide our actions," Alex stated. "We must uphold ethical principles in our use of technology, ensuring that our decisions and actions are guided by integrity, transparency, and accountability. By prioritizing ethics, we can build trust with our stakeholders and demonstrate our commitment to responsible leadership."

Promoting Data Privacy

Alex emphasized the importance of promoting data privacy and respecting the rights of individuals to control their personal information, particularly in the era of increased data collection and analysis.

"Data privacy is paramount," Alex declared. "We must respect the rights of individuals to control their personal information and comply with applicable data protection laws and regulations. By prioritizing data privacy, we can build trust with our customers and stakeholders and mitigate the risk of regulatory penalties and reputational damage."

Investing in Cybersecurity Education and Training

To mitigate cybersecurity risks, Alex committed to investing in cybersecurity education and training for employees, equipping them with the knowledge and skills needed to identify and respond to cyber threats effectively.

"Our employees are our first line of defense," Alex noted. "We must provide comprehensive cybersecurity education and training to ensure that our team members are aware of the latest threats and best practices for protecting against them. By investing in cybersecurity education, we can strengthen our organization's resilience to cyber threats and minimize the risk of data breaches."

Collaborating with Industry Partners

Alex stressed the importance of collaborating with industry partners and stakeholders to share information and best practices for cybersecurity and ethical considerations.

"Cybersecurity is a collective effort," Alex affirmed. "We must collaborate with industry partners, government agencies, and other stakeholders to share information and best practices for cybersecurity and ethical considerations. By working together, we can strengthen our collective resilience to cyber threats and uphold the highest standards of ethical conduct."

Conclusion

As the meeting came to a close, the leadership team left the cybersecurity center with a renewed commitment to prioritizing cybersecurity and ethical considerations in all aspects of technology and innovation. Armed with a clear understanding of the importance of safeguarding data and upholding ethical principles, they were ready to lead InovaTech into a future defined by integrity, transparency, and trust.

Case Studies of Tech-Driven Leadership

In the dynamic boardroom of InovaTech, Alex Carter stood before the leadership team, ready to delve into real-world examples of tech-driven leadership. Today's focus: exploring case studies of organizations and companies that have successfully leveraged technology and innovation to drive transformative change and achieve remarkable success.

Setting the Stage

"Good morning, everyone," Alex greeted, his voice filled with anticipation. "Today, we have the opportunity to draw inspiration from real-world examples of tech-driven leadership—organizations and companies that have embraced innovation and leveraged technology to redefine their industries and create lasting impact. By studying these case studies, we can uncover valuable insights and best practices that will guide our own journey of technological innovation and leadership."

Case Study 1: Amazon

Alex began by highlighting Amazon's remarkable journey from an online bookstore to a global powerhouse in e-commerce, cloud computing, and digital streaming.

"Amazon's story is a testament to the power of innovation and relentless customer focus," Alex noted. "By leveraging technology to optimize operations, personalize customer experiences, and drive continuous innovation, Amazon has revolutionized the retail industry and set new standards for customer service and convenience."

Case Study 2: Tesla

Next, Alex explored Tesla's groundbreaking innovations in electric vehicles, renewable energy, and autonomous driving technology.

"Tesla's vision of a sustainable future has reshaped the automotive industry," Alex affirmed. "By investing in research and development, pushing the boundaries of battery technology, and pioneering autonomous driving capabilities, Tesla has transformed the way we think about transportation and sustainability."

Case Study 3: Microsoft

Alex highlighted Microsoft's evolution from a software company to a leader in cloud computing, artificial intelligence, and productivity tools.

"Microsoft's commitment to innovation and collaboration has fueled its success in the digital age," Alex stated. "By embracing cloud computing and artificial intelligence, Microsoft has empowered businesses of all sizes to leverage technology to drive growth, productivity, and innovation."

Case Study 4: Airbnb

Lastly, Alex explored Airbnb's disruptive impact on the hospitality industry through its innovative platform for short-term rentals and experiences.

"Airbnb's platform has democratized travel and hospitality, empowering individuals to monetize their spaces and create unique experiences for travelers around the world," Alex observed. "By harnessing the power of technology and the sharing economy, Airbnb has redefined the way we travel and experience new destinations."

Conclusion

As the meeting came to a close, the leadership team left the boardroom with a newfound appreciation for the transformative power of technology and innovation in driving organizational success. Inspired by the case studies of tech-driven leadership, they were ready to apply the lessons learned to their own journey of innovation and leadership at InovaTech, confident in their ability to harness the power of technology to create value and drive meaningful change.

6

Chapter 6: Empowering and Inspiring Teams

Identifying and Nurturing Talent

In the vibrant workspace of InovaTech's talent development center, Alex Carter stood before the leadership team, ready to explore the transformative impact of identifying and nurturing talent within the organization. Today's focus: understanding the importance of recognizing potential and fostering growth to empower and inspire teams to achieve greatness.

Setting the Stage

"Good afternoon, everyone," Alex greeted, his voice filled with enthusiasm. "Today, we embark on a journey to unlock the potential of our greatest asset—our people. By identifying and nurturing talent within our organization, we can cultivate a culture of excellence, innovation, and collaboration that propels us toward our shared goals."

Recognizing Potential

Alex began by emphasizing the importance of recognizing potential in individuals, regardless of their background or experience.

"Potential knows no bounds," Alex affirmed. "We must look beyond resumes and titles to identify individuals with the passion, drive, and potential to excel within our organization. By recognizing and nurturing talent at all levels, we can unlock new opportunities for growth and innovation."

Investing in Development

Next, Alex highlighted the importance of investing in the development of talent through training, mentorship, and professional development opportunities.

"Development is key to unlocking potential," Alex noted. "We must invest in the growth and development of our team members, providing them with the resources, support, and guidance they need to thrive and reach their full potential. By fostering a culture of continuous learning and development, we can empower our team to achieve greatness."

Providing Mentorship and Support

Alex stressed the importance of providing mentorship and support to individuals as they navigate their career paths within the organization.

"Mentorship is a powerful catalyst for growth," Alex stated.

"We must pair individuals with mentors who can provide guidance, support, and valuable insights as they navigate their careers within our organization. By fostering meaningful mentorship relationships, we can accelerate the development of talent and cultivate future leaders."

Creating Opportunities for Growth

To empower individuals to reach their full potential, Alex committed to creating opportunities for growth and advancement within the organization.

"Growth is essential for fulfillment," Alex affirmed. "We must create pathways for career advancement and opportunities for individuals to take on new challenges, develop new skills, and pursue their passions within our organization. By creating a culture of opportunity and growth, we can inspire our team to reach new heights of excellence."

Fostering a Culture of Inclusion and Diversity

Lastly, Alex emphasized the importance of fostering a culture of inclusion and diversity to attract and retain top talent from diverse backgrounds and perspectives.

"Diversity drives innovation," Alex declared. "We must embrace diversity and inclusion as core values within our organization, creating an environment where all individuals feel valued, empowered, and supported. By harnessing the power of diverse perspectives and experiences, we can drive innovation, creativity, and excellence within our team."

Conclusion

As the meeting came to a close, the leadership team left the talent development center with a renewed commitment to identifying and nurturing talent within the organization. Inspired by the potential of their team members, they were ready to empower and inspire their teams to achieve greatness, confident in their ability to cultivate a culture of excellence, innovation, and collaboration at InovaTech.

Delegating Effectively: Trust and Accountability

In the bustling workspace of InovaTech's project management hub, Alex Carter stood before the leadership team, ready to explore the transformative power of effective delegation, built on trust and accountability. Today's focus: understanding how delegating responsibilities empowers team members and fosters a culture of trust and accountability within the organization.

Setting the Stage

"Good morning, everyone," Alex greeted, his voice resonating with authority and warmth. "Today, we delve into the art of effective delegation—a cornerstone of leadership that empowers individuals, fosters collaboration, and drives organizational success. By delegating effectively, we can unlock the full potential of our team members and cultivate a culture of trust and accountability that propels us toward our goals."

Empowering Through Delegation

Alex began by emphasizing the importance of empowering team members through delegation, entrusting them with meaningful responsibilities and opportunities to contribute to the organization's success.

"Empowerment begins with trust," Alex affirmed. "We must delegate authority and responsibility to our team members, giving them the autonomy and ownership to make decisions, take initiative, and drive projects forward. By empowering our team through delegation, we demonstrate our confidence in their abilities and create opportunities for growth and development."

Building Trust

Next, Alex highlighted the crucial role of trust in effective delegation, emphasizing the need to establish clear expectations, communicate openly, and demonstrate integrity and reliability in all interactions.

"Trust is the foundation of effective delegation," Alex noted. "We must build trust with our team members through open communication, transparency, and consistency in our actions. By establishing trust, we create a supportive environment where team members feel empowered to take on new challenges and make decisions with confidence."

Fostering Accountability

Alex stressed the importance of fostering accountability in delegation, setting clear goals and expectations, and holding team members accountable for their actions and outcomes.

"Accountability is essential for success," Alex declared. "We must set clear goals, define expectations, and establish metrics for success in delegation. By holding ourselves and our team members accountable for achieving results, we create a culture of accountability that drives performance and ensures that everyone is aligned with our organizational goals."

Providing Support and Guidance

To facilitate effective delegation, Alex committed to providing support and guidance to team members, offering resources, feedback, and mentorship to help them succeed in their delegated roles.

"Support is essential for growth," Alex affirmed. "We must provide our team members with the support and guidance they need to succeed in their delegated roles, offering resources, feedback, and mentorship to help them overcome challenges and achieve their goals. By providing support and guidance, we empower our team members to excel and contribute to our collective success."

Celebrating Success and Learning from Failure

Finally, Alex emphasized the importance of celebrating success and learning from failure in delegation, recognizing and rewarding achievements while fostering a culture of continuous improvement and innovation.

"Success is a team effort," Alex stated. "We must celebrate the achievements of our team members, recognizing their contributions and successes in delegation. At the same time, we must embrace failure as an opportunity for learning and growth, encouraging our team to experiment, take risks, and learn from their experiences. By celebrating success and learning from failure, we foster a culture of resilience, innovation, and continuous improvement within our organization."

Conclusion

As the meeting came to a close, the leadership team left the project management hub with a renewed appreciation for the transformative power of effective delegation, built on trust and accountability. Inspired by the potential of empowering their team members, they were ready to delegate responsibilities with confidence, knowing that they were fostering a culture of trust, accountability, and collaboration at InovaTech.

Building High-Performing Teams

In the collaborative atmosphere of InovaTech's team development center, Alex Carter stood before the leadership team, poised to explore the essential elements of building high-performing teams. Today's focus: understanding how to cultivate a culture of collaboration, communication, and cohesion that drives excellence and innovation within the organization.

Setting the Stage

"Good afternoon, everyone," Alex greeted, his voice filled with energy and determination. "Today, we embark on a journey to unlock the secrets of building high-performing teams—a cornerstone of organizational success. By fostering a culture of collaboration, communication, and cohesion, we can harness the collective talents and strengths of our team members to achieve extraordinary results and drive innovation."

Fostering Collaboration

Alex began by emphasizing the importance of fostering collaboration within teams, encouraging open communication, knowledge sharing, and cross-functional cooperation.

"Collaboration is the heartbeat of high-performing teams," Alex affirmed. "We must break down silos within our organization and foster a culture of collaboration that encourages team members to share ideas, collaborate on projects, and leverage each other's strengths to achieve common goals."

Cultivating Communication

Next, Alex highlighted the crucial role of communication in building high-performing teams, emphasizing the need for clear, open, and transparent communication channels.

"Communication is the lifeblood of effective teamwork," Alex noted. "We must prioritize clear and transparent communication within our teams, ensuring that everyone is aligned with goals, expectations, and project timelines. By cultivating a culture of open communication, we can minimize misunderstandings, foster trust, and maximize productivity."

Building Cohesion

Alex stressed the importance of building cohesion within teams, creating a sense of belonging and camaraderie that fosters mutual support and collaboration.

"Cohesion is the glue that holds teams together," Alex declared. "We must create opportunities for team bonding and relationship-building, fostering a sense of belonging and camaraderie that motivates team members to support and collaborate with one another. By building cohesion, we can strengthen team dynamics and drive collective success."

Embracing Diversity

To maximize the potential of high-performing teams, Alex emphasized the importance of embracing diversity and inclusion, recognizing and valuing the unique perspectives and contributions of each team member.

"Diversity is our strength," Alex affirmed. "We must embrace diversity and inclusion within our teams, recognizing that diverse perspectives lead to better decision-making, innovation, and problem-solving. By embracing diversity, we can create high-performing teams that are resilient, adaptive, and capable of achieving extraordinary results."

Fostering a Culture of Excellence

Finally, Alex committed to fostering a culture of excellence within teams, setting high standards for performance, and providing support and resources to help team members achieve their full potential.

"Excellence is our benchmark," Alex stated. "We must set high standards for performance within our teams, providing the support and resources needed to help team members achieve their goals. By fostering a culture of excellence, we can inspire our teams to strive for greatness and achieve extraordinary results."

Conclusion

As the meeting drew to a close, the leadership team left the team development center with a renewed commitment to building high-performing teams within InovaTech. Inspired by the potential of collaboration, communication, and cohesion, they were ready to cultivate a culture of excellence and innovation that would drive the organization to new heights of success.

Motivational Techniques for Innovative Thinking

In the vibrant innovation lab of InovaTech, Alex Carter stood before the leadership team, ready to explore motivational techniques that ignite innovative thinking within teams. Today's focus: understanding how to inspire creativity, curiosity, and risk-taking to drive breakthrough innovation and propel the organization forward.

Setting the Stage

"Good morning, everyone," Alex greeted, his voice alive with enthusiasm. "Today, we delve into the realm of motivational techniques for innovative thinking—a crucial aspect of fostering creativity, experimentation, and bold thinking within our teams. By inspiring our team members to embrace innovation, we can unlock new possibilities, drive transformative change, and position InovaTech as a leader in our industry."

Cultivating Curiosity

Alex began by emphasizing the importance of cultivating curiosity within teams, encouraging team members to ask questions, explore new ideas, and challenge the status quo.

"Curiosity is the spark of innovation," Alex affirmed. "We must cultivate a culture of curiosity within our teams, encouraging team members to question assumptions, explore new perspectives, and seek out innovative solutions to challenges. By fostering curiosity, we can ignite the creative spark that drives breakthrough innovation."

Encouraging Risk-Taking

Next, Alex highlighted the importance of encouraging risk-taking within teams, empowering team members to take calculated risks and explore new opportunities without fear of failure.

"Risk-taking is the essence of innovation," Alex noted. "We must create a safe space for experimentation within our teams, where team members are encouraged to take calculated risks, test new ideas, and learn from failure. By embracing risk-taking, we can inspire bold thinking and drive breakthrough innovation."

Providing Autonomy and Flexibility

Alex stressed the importance of providing autonomy and flexibility to team members, empowering them to pursue projects and initiatives that align with their passions and strengths.

"Autonomy fuels innovation," Alex declared. "We must empower our team members to take ownership of their work, providing them with the autonomy and flexibility to pursue projects and initiatives that inspire them. By providing autonomy, we can unleash the full potential of our team members and foster a culture of innovation and creativity."

Recognizing and Rewarding Innovation

To incentivize innovative thinking, Alex committed to recognizing and rewarding team members who demonstrate creativity, initiative, and a willingness to challenge the status quo.

"Innovation deserves recognition," Alex affirmed. "We must celebrate and reward team members who demonstrate innovative thinking and drive positive change within our organization. By recognizing and rewarding innovation, we reinforce its importance and inspire others to embrace creative thinking and experimentation."

Fostering Collaboration and Cross-Pollination

Lastly, Alex emphasized the importance of fostering collaboration and cross-pollination of ideas within teams, encouraging diverse perspectives and interdisciplinary approaches to problem-solving.

"Collaboration breeds innovation," Alex stated. "We must create opportunities for collaboration and cross-pollination of ideas within our teams, bringing together individuals from diverse backgrounds and disciplines to tackle complex challenges. By fostering collaboration, we can leverage the collective wisdom and creativity of our team members to drive breakthrough innovation."

Conclusion

As the meeting came to a close, the leadership team left the innovation lab with a renewed commitment to inspiring innovative thinking within their teams. Inspired by the potential of curiosity, risk-taking, and collaboration, they were ready to cultivate a culture of innovation and creativity that would propel InovaTech to new heights of success in the rapidly evolving landscape of technology and business.

Coaching and Mentorship: Developing Future Leaders

In the serene confines of InovaTech's leadership development center, Alex Carter stood before the leadership team, ready to explore the transformative power of coaching and mentorship in developing future leaders. Today's focus: understanding how to nurture talent, foster growth, and cultivate leadership potential within the organization.

Setting the Stage

"Good afternoon, everyone," Alex greeted, his voice resonating with warmth and wisdom. "Today, we embark on a journey to unlock the potential of our future leaders—a journey guided by the principles of coaching and mentorship. By investing in the development of our team members and providing them with the support and guidance they need to succeed, we can cultivate a new generation of leaders who will drive innovation, inspire excellence, and lead InovaTech into the future."

Nurturing Talent Through Coaching

Alex began by emphasizing the importance of nurturing talent through coaching, providing individuals with personalized guidance, feedback, and support to help them reach their full potential.

"Coaching is the key to unlocking talent," Alex affirmed. "We must invest in coaching programs that provide our team members with personalized guidance and support, helping them identify their strengths, address their weaknesses, and develop the skills and competencies needed to succeed in their roles. By nurturing talent through coaching, we can empower our team members to achieve greatness and drive organizational success."

Providing Mentorship and Guidance

Next, Alex highlighted the crucial role of mentorship in developing future leaders, pairing individuals with experienced leaders who can provide valuable insights, advice, and support as they navigate their career paths.

"Mentorship is a guiding light," Alex noted. "We must establish mentorship programs that pair our team members with experienced leaders who can provide them with valuable advice, insights, and support as they progress in their careers. By providing mentorship and guidance, we can accelerate the development of future leaders and ensure that they are equipped with the knowledge and skills needed to succeed."

Fostering Growth Mindsets

Alex stressed the importance of fostering growth mindsets within the organization, encouraging team members to embrace challenges, learn from failure, and continuously improve themselves and their skills.

"Growth begins with mindset," Alex declared. "We must cultivate a culture of growth and learning within our organization, encouraging our team members to embrace challenges, seek out opportunities for development, and continuously strive to improve themselves and their skills. By fostering growth mindsets, we can create a culture of resilience, adaptability, and continuous improvement that drives organizational success."

Empowering Leadership Opportunities

To develop future leaders, Alex committed to providing leadership opportunities and responsibilities to team members, empowering them to take on new challenges and develop their leadership skills in real-world settings.

"Leadership is a journey," Alex affirmed. "We must provide our team members with opportunities to take on leadership roles and responsibilities, empowering them to lead projects, teams, and initiatives that stretch their abilities and develop their leadership skills. By empowering leadership opportunities, we can cultivate a new generation of leaders who are prepared to take on the challenges of tomorrow."

Celebrating Success and Progress

Lastly, Alex emphasized the importance of celebrating the success and progress of future leaders, recognizing their achievements and milestones as they progress in their leadership journey.

"Success deserves recognition," Alex stated. "We must celebrate the achievements and progress of our future leaders, recognizing their contributions and milestones as they develop their leadership skills and make a positive impact within our organization. By celebrating success, we reinforce the importance of leadership development and inspire others to follow in their footsteps."

Conclusion

As the meeting came to a close, the leadership team left the leadership development center with a renewed commitment to investing in the development of future leaders within InovaTech. Inspired by the potential of coaching and mentorship, they were ready to cultivate a new generation of leaders who would drive innovation, inspire excellence, and lead the organization to new heights of success.

Celebrating Successes and Recognizing Contributions

In the lively gathering space of InovaTech's communal area, Alex Carter stood before the leadership team, prepared to delve into the importance of celebrating successes and recognizing contributions within the organization. Today's focus: understanding how acknowledgment and appreciation inspire motivation, foster team spirit, and drive continuous excellence.

Setting the Stage

"Good morning, everyone," Alex greeted, his voice echoing with anticipation and warmth. "Today, we come together to honor the achievements and contributions of our team members—a celebration of the dedication, creativity, and hard work that propel InovaTech forward. By taking the time to acknowledge and appreciate the successes of our team, we can foster a culture of positivity, motivation, and collective pride that fuels our continued success."

Honoring Achievements

Alex began by emphasizing the importance of honoring achievements within the organization, recognizing milestones, accomplishments, and breakthroughs that contribute to the organization's success.

"Achievement is the result of dedication and effort," Alex affirmed. "We must take the time to honor the achievements of our team members, celebrating milestones, accomplishments, and breakthroughs that drive our organization forward. By recognizing and celebrating success, we reinforce the value of hard work, dedication, and innovation that defines our culture at InovaTech."

Recognizing Contributions

Next, Alex highlighted the crucial role of recognizing individual contributions within teams, acknowledging the unique talents, skills, and efforts that each team member brings to the table.

"Contribution is the foundation of teamwork," Alex noted. "We must recognize and appreciate the contributions of our team members, acknowledging their unique talents, skills, and efforts that contribute to the success of our projects and initiatives. By recognizing individual contributions, we foster a sense of belonging, appreciation, and camaraderie within our teams."

Inspiring Motivation and Engagement

Alex stressed the importance of inspiring motivation and engagement through celebration and recognition, energizing team members and fueling their passion for excellence.

"Motivation is the fuel of success," Alex declared. "We must inspire motivation and engagement within our teams through celebration and recognition, energizing our team members and fueling their passion for excellence. By celebrating successes and recognizing contributions, we inspire our team members to continue pushing boundaries, challenging themselves, and striving for greatness."

Fostering Team Spirit

To cultivate a strong sense of unity and camaraderie within the organization, Alex committed to fostering team spirit through collective celebration and recognition.

"Team spirit binds us together," Alex affirmed. "We must foster a culture of unity and camaraderie within our organization, celebrating successes and recognizing contributions as a collective team. By coming together to celebrate our achievements, we strengthen our bonds, build trust, and reinforce our shared commitment to excellence."

Cultivating a Culture of Appreciation

Lastly, Alex emphasized the importance of cultivating a culture of appreciation within the organization, where recognition and acknowledgment are woven into the fabric of everyday interactions.

"Appreciation is contagious," Alex stated. "We must cultivate a culture of appreciation within our organization, where recognition and acknowledgment are woven into the fabric of everyday interactions. By expressing gratitude and appreciation for the efforts of our team members, we create a positive and supportive environment where everyone feels valued, respected, and motivated to succeed."

Conclusion

As the meeting came to a close, the leadership team left the communal area with a renewed commitment to celebrating successes and recognizing contributions within InovaTech. Inspired by the power of acknowledgment and appreciation, they were ready to cultivate a culture of positivity, motivation, and collective pride that would drive continuous excellence and success within the organization.

7

Chapter 7: Driving Innovation Through Diversity and Inclusion

The Business Case for Diversity

In the modern and inclusive meeting room of InovaTech, Alex Carter stood before the leadership team, ready to explore the compelling business case for diversity and inclusion. Today's focus: understanding how embracing diversity drives innovation, enhances decision-making, and fuels organizational success.

Setting the Stage

"Good afternoon, everyone," Alex greeted, his voice resonating with conviction and purpose. "Today, we embark on a journey to unlock the power of diversity and inclusion—a journey guided by the belief that diversity is not just a moral imperative but a strategic advantage. By embracing diversity and inclusion within our organization, we can drive innovation, foster creativity, and unlock new opportunities for growth and success."

Exploring the Benefits of Diversity

Alex began by highlighting the numerous benefits of diversity within organizations, including increased innovation, enhanced decision-making, and improved financial performance.

"Diversity is a catalyst for innovation," Alex affirmed. "By bringing together individuals from diverse backgrounds, experiences, and perspectives, we can generate a wider range of ideas, insights, and solutions that drive innovation and creativity within our organization. By embracing diversity, we can unlock new opportunities for growth and success."

Enhancing Decision-Making

Next, Alex emphasized the importance of diversity in enhancing decision-making processes, reducing the risks of groupthink and promoting critical thinking and problem-solving.

"Diversity leads to better decisions," Alex noted. "By incorporating diverse perspectives into our decision-making processes, we can challenge assumptions, avoid blind spots, and make more informed and effective decisions. By embracing diversity, we can harness the collective wisdom and expertise of our team members to drive organizational success."

Improving Financial Performance

Alex highlighted the link between diversity and improved financial performance, citing numerous studies that have shown a positive correlation between diverse leadership teams and profitability.

"Diversity drives financial success," Alex declared. "By fostering diversity and inclusion within our organization, we can tap into new markets, better understand customer needs, and drive innovation that leads to increased revenue and profitability. By embracing diversity, we can create a competitive advantage that propels us ahead of our peers."

Attracting and Retaining Talent

To attract and retain top talent, Alex stressed the importance of creating an inclusive workplace culture that values and respects individuals from all backgrounds.

"Inclusion is the key to talent retention," Alex affirmed. "By creating an inclusive workplace culture where all team members feel valued, respected, and empowered to contribute their unique perspectives and talents, we can attract and retain top talent from diverse backgrounds. By embracing diversity and inclusion, we can build a strong and resilient team that drives organizational success."

Conclusion

As the meeting came to a close, the leadership team left the meeting room with a renewed commitment to driving innovation through diversity and inclusion within InovaTech.

Inspired by the compelling business case for diversity, they were ready to embrace diversity as a strategic advantage, knowing that by fostering a culture of inclusion and belonging, they could unlock new opportunities for growth, success, and innovation within the organization.

Inclusive Leadership: Practices and Principles

In the progressive workspace of InovaTech's leadership development center, Alex Carter stood before the leadership team, poised to explore the essential principles and practices of inclusive leadership. Today's focus: understanding how inclusive leadership fosters a culture of belonging, respect, and innovation within the organization.

Setting the Stage

"Good morning, everyone," Alex greeted, his voice filled with warmth and determination. "Today, we delve into the heart of inclusive leadership—a leadership style that values and respects individuals from all backgrounds and perspectives. By embracing inclusive leadership practices and principles, we can foster a culture of belonging, empower our team members, and drive innovation and success within our organization."

Leading by Example

Alex began by emphasizing the importance of leading by example, demonstrating inclusive behaviors and fostering a culture of respect and belonging within the organization.

"Leadership sets the tone," Alex affirmed. "We must lead by

example, demonstrating inclusive behaviors and values in our interactions with others. By showing respect, empathy, and openness to diverse perspectives, we create a culture where all team members feel valued, respected, and empowered to contribute their unique talents and insights."

Embracing Diversity of Thought

Next, Alex highlighted the importance of embracing diversity of thought within teams, encouraging open dialogue, and constructive dissent to drive innovation and creativity.

"Diversity of thought fuels innovation," Alex noted. "We must embrace diverse perspectives and ideas within our teams, encouraging open dialogue and constructive dissent that challenges assumptions and drives innovative thinking. By embracing diversity of thought, we can unlock new opportunities for growth and success within our organization."

Creating Inclusive Processes and Policies

Alex stressed the importance of creating inclusive processes and policies within the organization, ensuring that all team members have equal opportunities to contribute and succeed.

"Inclusion starts with processes and policies," Alex declared. "We must review and revise our processes and policies to ensure that they are fair, equitable, and inclusive of all team members. By removing barriers to participation and advancement, we can create a more inclusive workplace where everyone has the opportunity to thrive and succeed."

Fostering Psychological Safety

To cultivate a culture of belonging and innovation, Alex committed to fostering psychological safety within teams, creating an environment where team members feel comfortable taking risks and expressing their ideas without fear of judgment or retribution.

"Psychological safety is essential for innovation," Alex affirmed. "We must create a culture of psychological safety within our teams, where team members feel empowered to speak up, take risks, and share their ideas without fear of criticism or punishment. By fostering psychological safety, we can unleash the full potential of our team members and drive innovation and creativity."

Championing Diversity and Inclusion

Lastly, Alex emphasized the importance of championing diversity and inclusion as core values within the organization, ensuring that they are embedded into the fabric of everyday operations and decision-making processes.

"Diversity and inclusion are our guiding principles," Alex stated. "We must champion diversity and inclusion as core values within our organization, ensuring that they are reflected in our hiring practices, team dynamics, and organizational culture. By championing diversity and inclusion, we can create a workplace where everyone feels valued, respected, and empowered to succeed."

Conclusion

As the meeting came to a close, the leadership team left the leadership development center with a renewed commitment to practicing inclusive leadership within InovaTech. Inspired by the principles and practices of inclusive leadership, they were ready to foster a culture of belonging, respect, and innovation that would drive success and excellence within the organization.

Harnessing Diverse Perspectives for Innovation

In the dynamic collaboration space of InovaTech's innovation hub, Alex Carter stood before the leadership team, prepared to explore the transformative power of harnessing diverse perspectives for innovation. Today's focus: understanding how embracing diversity of thought drives creativity, problem-solving, and innovation within the organization.

Setting the Stage

"Good afternoon, everyone," Alex greeted, his voice filled with energy and enthusiasm. "Today, we embark on a journey to unlock the potential of diverse perspectives—a journey guided by the belief that innovation thrives on the collision of ideas and the convergence of diverse viewpoints. By embracing diversity of thought within our organization, we can unlock new opportunities, solve complex challenges, and drive transformative innovation that propels us ahead of our competitors."

Embracing Diversity of Thought

Alex began by emphasizing the importance of embracing diversity of thought within teams, recognizing the unique perspectives, experiences, and insights that each team member brings to the table.

"Diversity of thought is our greatest asset," Alex affirmed. "We must embrace the diverse perspectives and experiences of our team members, recognizing that innovation thrives on the collision of ideas and the convergence of diverse viewpoints. By embracing diversity of thought, we can challenge assumptions, break down barriers, and unlock new possibilities for innovation and growth."

Encouraging Open Dialogue and Debate

Next, Alex highlighted the importance of encouraging open dialogue and constructive debate within teams, creating a culture where diverse perspectives are valued and respected.

"Dialogue drives innovation," Alex noted. "We must encourage open dialogue and constructive debate within our teams, creating a culture where diverse perspectives are welcomed and respected. By fostering an environment where team members feel comfortable expressing their ideas and challenging the status quo, we can spark creativity, drive innovation, and find novel solutions to complex problems."

Leveraging Cross-Functional Collaboration

Alex stressed the importance of leveraging cross-functional collaboration to harness diverse perspectives and expertise from across the organization.

"Collaboration fuels innovation," Alex declared. "We must leverage cross-functional collaboration to bring together individuals from diverse backgrounds and disciplines, tapping into their unique perspectives and expertise to drive innovation. By breaking down silos and fostering collaboration across teams, we can harness the collective intelligence of our organization and generate innovative solutions that address the evolving needs of our customers and stakeholders."

Promoting Diversity in Decision-Making

To ensure that diverse perspectives are incorporated into decision-making processes, Alex committed to promoting diversity in leadership and decision-making roles within the organization.

"Diversity drives better decisions," Alex affirmed. "We must promote diversity in leadership and decision-making roles within our organization, ensuring that diverse perspectives are represented at every level of the organization. By incorporating diverse viewpoints into our decision-making processes, we can make more informed and effective decisions that drive innovation and success."

Cultivating a Culture of Innovation

Lastly, Alex emphasized the importance of cultivating a culture of innovation that values and celebrates diverse perspectives and contributions.

"Innovation is our mindset," Alex stated. "We must cultivate a culture of innovation that values and celebrates diverse perspectives and contributions, recognizing that innovation thrives when all team members are empowered to contribute their unique talents and insights. By fostering a culture of innovation, we can unleash the full potential of our organization and drive transformative change that propels us ahead of our competitors."

Conclusion

As the meeting came to a close, the leadership team left the innovation hub with a renewed commitment to harnessing diverse perspectives for innovation within InovaTech. Inspired by the potential of diversity of thought, they were ready to embrace new ideas, challenge assumptions, and drive transformative innovation that would propel the organization to new heights of success.

Addressing Biases and Barriers in the Workplace

In the inclusive and supportive environment of InovaTech's diversity workshop, Alex Carter stood before the leadership team, prepared to tackle the crucial topic of addressing biases and barriers in the workplace. Today's focus: understanding how unconscious biases and systemic barriers can impede diversity and inclusion efforts, and exploring strategies to overcome them.

Setting the Stage

"Good morning, everyone," Alex greeted, his voice calm yet determined. "Today, we confront a challenging yet essential aspect of our journey towards diversity and inclusion: addressing biases and barriers that hinder our progress. By acknowledging and addressing these obstacles head-on, we can create a more inclusive workplace where all team members feel valued, respected, and empowered to contribute their unique perspectives and talents."

Recognizing Unconscious Biases

Alex began by highlighting the existence of unconscious biases and their impact on decision-making processes, hiring practices, and workplace interactions.

"Biases shape our perceptions," Alex noted. "We must recognize that we all have unconscious biases that influence our judgments and behaviors, often without our awareness. By acknowledging the presence of biases, we can begin to mitigate their impact and create a more inclusive and equitable workplace for all."

Challenging Stereotypes and Assumptions

Next, Alex emphasized the importance of challenging stereotypes and assumptions that perpetuate bias and discrimination within the workplace.

"Stereotypes limit potential," Alex declared. "We must challenge stereotypes and assumptions that reinforce bias and discrimination, creating a culture where all team members are judged based on their merits and contributions rather than their background or identity. By fostering an environment of inclusion and respect, we can create opportunities for all team members to thrive and succeed."

Mitigating Systemic Barriers

Alex highlighted the presence of systemic barriers that disproportionately affect certain groups within the organization, such as lack of access to resources, opportunities for advancement, or representation in leadership roles.

"Systems shape experiences," Alex affirmed. "We must identify and mitigate systemic barriers that perpetuate inequality and limit opportunities for certain groups within our organization. By implementing policies and practices that promote fairness, equity, and inclusion, we can create a more level playing field where all team members have the opportunity to succeed."

Providing Diversity and Inclusion Training

To raise awareness and build skills for addressing biases and barriers, Alex committed to providing diversity and inclusion training for all team members.

"Education empowers change," Alex stated. "We must provide diversity and inclusion training for all team members, equipping them with the knowledge and skills needed to recognize and address biases and barriers in the workplace. By fostering awareness and understanding, we can create a more inclusive and equitable workplace culture that values diversity and empowers all team members to succeed."

Creating Accountability and Transparency

Lastly, Alex emphasized the importance of creating accountability and transparency around diversity and inclusion efforts, setting measurable goals and benchmarks for progress.

"Accountability drives progress," Alex affirmed. "We must create accountability and transparency around our diversity and inclusion efforts, setting measurable goals and benchmarks for progress. By holding ourselves and each other accountable, we can ensure that diversity and inclusion remain a priority and drive meaningful change within our organization."

Conclusion

As the workshop came to a close, the leadership team left with a renewed commitment to addressing biases and barriers in the workplace within InovaTech. Inspired by the potential for positive change, they were ready to take action to create a more inclusive and equitable workplace where all team members feel valued, respected, and empowered to succeed.

Creating an Inclusive Environment: Policies and Practices

In the progressive atmosphere of InovaTech's diversity and inclusion task force meeting, Alex Carter stood before the leadership team, ready to delve into the critical topic of creating an inclusive environment through policies and practices. Today's focus: understanding how organizational policies and practices can shape culture and foster inclusivity within the workplace.

Setting the Stage

"Good afternoon, everyone," Alex greeted, his voice resonating with purpose and conviction. "Today, we embark on a journey to explore the power of organizational policies and practices in creating an inclusive environment where all team members feel valued, respected, and empowered to bring their authentic selves to work. By implementing policies and practices that promote diversity, equity, and inclusion, we can cultivate a culture of belonging and innovation that drives success within our organization."

Implementing Diverse Hiring Practices

Alex began by emphasizing the importance of implementing diverse hiring practices to attract and retain talent from all backgrounds.

"Our hiring practices shape our workforce," Alex noted. "We must implement diverse hiring practices that attract and retain talent from diverse backgrounds, ensuring that our workforce reflects the rich tapestry of perspectives and experiences in our society. By casting a wide net and actively seeking out diverse candidates, we can build a stronger and more resilient team that drives innovation and success."

Establishing Equal Opportunities for Advancement

Next, Alex highlighted the importance of establishing equal opportunities for advancement within the organization, ensuring that all team members have the chance to grow and succeed based on their merits and contributions.

"Opportunities drive ambition," Alex declared. "We must establish equal opportunities for advancement within our organization, ensuring that all team members have the chance to grow and succeed based on their talents and potential. By removing barriers to advancement and providing support and mentorship, we can create a culture where everyone has the opportunity to reach their full potential."

Promoting Work-Life Balance and Flexibility

Alex stressed the importance of promoting work-life balance and flexibility to accommodate the diverse needs and responsibilities of team members.

"Balance breeds well-being," Alex affirmed. "We must promote work-life balance and flexibility within our organization, recognizing that each team member has unique needs and responsibilities outside of work. By offering flexible work arrangements and support for work-life balance, we can create an environment where everyone feels valued, respected, and able to thrive both personally and professionally."

Providing Diversity and Inclusion Training

To foster awareness and understanding of diversity and inclusion issues, Alex committed to providing ongoing training and education for all team members.

"Education empowers change," Alex stated. "We must provide diversity and inclusion training for all team members, equipping them with the knowledge and skills needed to create an inclusive and equitable workplace culture. By fostering awareness and understanding, we can challenge biases, address barriers, and create a more inclusive environment where everyone feels valued and respected."

Establishing Reporting Mechanisms for Discrimination and Harassment

Lastly, Alex emphasized the importance of establishing reporting mechanisms for discrimination and harassment, ensuring that all team members feel safe and supported in the workplace.

"Support breeds trust," Alex affirmed. "We must establish reporting mechanisms for discrimination and harassment, ensuring that all team members feel safe and supported in the workplace. By providing avenues for reporting and addressing incidents of discrimination and harassment, we can create a culture where everyone feels empowered to speak up and take action to ensure a respectful and inclusive environment for all."

Conclusion

As the meeting came to a close, the diversity and inclusion task force left with a renewed commitment to creating an inclusive environment through policies and practices within InovaTech. Inspired by the potential for positive change, they were ready to implement strategies and initiatives that would foster diversity, equity, and inclusion and drive success within the organization.

Success Stories: How Diversity Fuels Innovation

In the vibrant conference room of InovaTech's headquarters, Alex Carter stood before the leadership team, eager to share inspiring success stories that demonstrate how diversity fuels innovation. Today's focus: showcasing real-world examples of organizations that have leveraged diversity to drive creativity, problem-solving, and success.

Setting the Stage

"Good morning, everyone," Alex greeted, his voice filled with excitement and anticipation. "Today, I'm thrilled to share with you some success stories that illustrate the transformative power of diversity in driving innovation and success within organizations. These stories serve as inspiring examples of how embracing diversity can unlock new opportunities, challenge the status quo, and propel organizations ahead of their competitors."

Story 1: Airbnb

Alex began by sharing the story of Airbnb, a global online marketplace for lodging and experiences. He recounted how Airbnb's founders, Brian Chesky, Joe Gebbia, and Nathan Blecharczyk, recognized the potential for diversity to drive innovation and creativity within their organization.

"At Airbnb, diversity is celebrated as a core value," Alex explained. "The company actively seeks out employees from diverse backgrounds and experiences, recognizing that diversity fosters innovation and creativity. By embracing diversity, Airbnb has been able to develop innovative solutions that address the evolving needs of its global community of hosts and guests, propelling the company to unprecedented success in the sharing economy."

Story 2: Google

Next, Alex shared the story of Google, a multinational technology company known for its innovative products and services. He recounted how Google's commitment to diversity and inclusion has been integral to its success in driving innovation and shaping the future of technology.

"Google is a pioneer in diversity and inclusion," Alex noted. "The company understands that diverse teams are more innovative and better equipped to solve complex problems. By fostering a culture of inclusion where all voices are heard and valued, Google has been able to develop groundbreaking technologies that have transformed industries and changed the way we live and work."

Story 3: Johnson & Johnson

Lastly, Alex shared the story of Johnson & Johnson, a multinational corporation known for its pharmaceutical, medical devices, and consumer healthcare products. He recounted how Johnson & Johnson's commitment to diversity and inclusion has been a driving force behind its success in driving innovation and improving health outcomes for people around the world.

"Johnson & Johnson believes that diversity is essential to driving innovation and better serving its customers," Alex explained. "The company actively seeks out diverse perspectives and experiences to inform its product development and marketing strategies. By embracing diversity, Johnson & Johnson has been able to develop life-saving medications, medical devices, and consumer healthcare products that have made a positive impact on the lives of millions of people worldwide."

Conclusion

As the presentation came to a close, the leadership team left the conference room feeling inspired and energized by the success stories shared by Alex. They were reminded of the transformative power of diversity in driving innovation and success within organizations and were eager to continue their journey towards creating a more inclusive and equitable workplace culture within InovaTech.

8

Chapter 8: Navigating Global Leadership Challenges

Understanding Global Market Dynamics

In the sleek boardroom of InovaTech's headquarters, Alex Carter stood before the leadership team, prepared to delve into the complexities of navigating global leadership challenges. Today's focus: understanding the intricate dynamics of the global market and how they shape leadership strategies and decisions.

Setting the Stage

"Good morning, everyone," Alex greeted, his voice projecting confidence and authority. "As we expand our horizons and embrace new opportunities on the global stage, it's essential that we understand the dynamic landscape of the global market. Today, we'll explore the factors that influence global market dynamics and how they impact our leadership approach."

The Ever-Changing Global Landscape

Alex began by highlighting the ever-changing nature of the global market, shaped by factors such as economic trends, geopolitical shifts, and technological advancements.

"The global market is in a constant state of flux," Alex explained. "Economic trends, geopolitical tensions, and technological innovations all contribute to the dynamic nature of the global landscape. As leaders, it's crucial that we stay informed and adaptable, ready to navigate the challenges and seize the opportunities that arise."

Cultural Considerations

Next, Alex emphasized the importance of understanding cultural nuances and differences when operating in global markets.

"Cultural awareness is key," Alex noted. "Different cultures have different values, norms, and communication styles. As we expand into new markets, it's essential that we understand and respect these cultural differences. By embracing cultural diversity and adapting our approach accordingly, we can build trust and foster positive relationships with customers, partners, and stakeholders around the world."

Market Trends and Opportunities

Alex highlighted the importance of staying attuned to market trends and identifying emerging opportunities for growth and expansion.

"Market intelligence is critical," Alex affirmed. "By monitoring market trends and consumer behavior, we can identify emerging opportunities and position ourselves for success. Whether it's tapping into new markets, launching innovative products, or expanding our service offerings, staying ahead of the curve is essential in today's global economy."

Risk Management

Lastly, Alex stressed the importance of effective risk management strategies in mitigating potential challenges and uncertainties in the global market.

"Risk is inherent in global business," Alex stated. "From currency fluctuations to regulatory changes, there are numerous risks that we must navigate as global leaders. By implementing robust risk management strategies and contingency plans, we can minimize the impact of potential challenges and ensure the resilience of our operations."

Conclusion

As the discussion came to a close, the leadership team left the boardroom with a newfound appreciation for the complexities of navigating global leadership challenges. Inspired by Alex's insights, they were ready to embrace the opportunities and overcome the obstacles that lay ahead as they continued to expand and thrive in the global market.

Cultural Competence: Leading Across Borders

In the bustling conference room of InovaTech's international strategy department, Alex Carter stood before the leadership team, prepared to explore the importance of cultural competence in leading across borders. Today's focus: understanding how cultural differences influence leadership styles and strategies in the global arena.

Setting the Stage

"Good afternoon, everyone," Alex greeted, his tone welcoming yet authoritative. "As we expand our operations into new markets and collaborate with diverse teams around the world, it's crucial that we cultivate cultural competence as leaders. Today, we'll delve into the nuances of leading across borders and navigating cultural differences with respect and sensitivity."

Embracing Cultural Diversity

Alex began by emphasizing the value of embracing cultural diversity within the organization and recognizing the unique perspectives and contributions of team members from different cultural backgrounds.

"Cultural diversity enriches our organization," Alex affirmed. "By embracing diversity and fostering an inclusive environment where all voices are heard and respected, we can harness the collective wisdom and creativity of our global team. As leaders, it's essential that we celebrate cultural differences and create a culture of mutual respect and understanding."

Adapting Leadership Styles

Next, Alex highlighted the importance of adapting leadership styles to accommodate cultural differences and preferences.

"Flexibility is key," Alex noted. "Different cultures have different expectations and preferences when it comes to leadership. Some cultures value hierarchical structures and formal communication, while others prefer a more egalitarian and collaborative approach. As leaders, we must be adaptable and open-minded, tailoring our leadership style to fit the cultural context and preferences of our team members."

Building Trust and Relationships

Alex stressed the importance of building trust and relationships across cultural boundaries, recognizing that trust is the foundation of effective collaboration and teamwork.

"Trust is the currency of global business," Alex declared. "Building trust takes time and effort, especially across cultural boundaries. As leaders, we must invest in building strong relationships with our colleagues and partners around the world, demonstrating integrity, empathy, and cultural sensitivity in our interactions. By fostering trust and rapport, we can create a solid foundation for collaboration and success."

Communicating Effectively

Lastly, Alex emphasized the importance of effective communication in bridging cultural differences and avoiding misunderstandings.

"Communication is key," Alex affirmed. "Clear and transparent communication is essential in navigating cultural differences and building strong relationships. As leaders, we must be mindful of cultural nuances in communication styles and adapt our approach accordingly. By fostering open dialogue and active listening, we can ensure that our messages are understood and interpreted accurately across cultural boundaries."

Conclusion

As the discussion drew to a close, the leadership team left the conference room with a deeper understanding of the importance of cultural competence in leading across borders. Inspired by Alex's insights, they were ready to embrace cultural diversity, adapt their leadership styles, and foster trust and communication across cultural boundaries as they continued to navigate the complexities of the global market.

Global Leadership Strategies for Innovation

In the dynamic environment of InovaTech's innovation lab, Alex Carter stood before the leadership team, prepared to explore global leadership strategies for driving innovation. Today's focus: understanding how leaders can foster a culture of innovation across borders and leverage diverse perspectives to drive creative solutions and sustainable growth.

Setting the Stage

"Good morning, everyone," Alex greeted, his voice brimming with enthusiasm. "As we continue to expand our presence in the global market, it's essential that we develop innovative leadership strategies that transcend borders and harness the power of diversity. Today, we'll explore how leaders can cultivate a culture of innovation and drive creative solutions that propel us ahead of the competition."

Embracing Diversity in Innovation

Alex began by emphasizing the importance of embracing diversity as a catalyst for innovation, recognizing that diverse perspectives lead to more creative and robust solutions.

"Diversity fuels innovation," Alex affirmed. "By bringing together individuals from diverse backgrounds and experiences, we can unlock new perspectives, challenge assumptions, and drive creative solutions to complex problems. As leaders, it's essential that we create an environment where all team members feel empowered to contribute their unique insights and ideas."

Encouraging Risk-Taking and Experimentation

Next, Alex highlighted the importance of encouraging risk-taking and experimentation in driving innovation, recognizing that failure is an inevitable part of the innovation process.

"Risk leads to reward," Alex noted. "As leaders, we must create a culture where team members feel comfortable taking risks and experimenting with new ideas. By embracing a mindset of experimentation and learning from failure, we can foster a culture of innovation where bold ideas are celebrated and encouraged."

Leveraging Technology and Collaboration

Alex stressed the importance of leveraging technology and collaboration to drive innovation across borders, recognizing that technology enables seamless communication and collaboration among global teams.

"Technology enables collaboration," Alex declared. "By leveraging digital tools and platforms, we can facilitate seamless communication and collaboration among our global teams. Whether it's virtual brainstorming sessions, cross-functional collaboration tools, or digital project management platforms, technology enables us to harness the collective intelligence and creativity of our global team."

Empowering Team Members

Lastly, Alex emphasized the importance of empowering team members to take ownership of the innovation process, recognizing that innovation thrives in environments where individuals feel empowered to take initiative and drive change.

"Empowerment drives innovation," Alex affirmed. "As leaders, it's essential that we empower our team members to take ownership of the innovation process and pursue bold ideas that challenge the status quo. By providing support, resources, and encouragement, we can unleash the full potential of our team and drive innovation that propels us ahead of the competition."

Conclusion

As the discussion came to a close, the leadership team left the innovation lab feeling inspired and energized by Alex's insights into global leadership strategies for innovation. They were ready to embrace diversity, encourage risk-taking and experimentation, leverage technology and collaboration, and empower team members to drive creative solutions that propel InovaTech to new heights of success in the global market.

Managing Remote and Distributed Teams

In the modern workspace of InovaTech's virtual collaboration hub, Alex Carter stood before the leadership team, prepared to tackle the complexities of managing remote and distributed teams. Today's focus: understanding the unique challenges and opportunities of leading teams across geographical boundaries and time zones.

Setting the Stage

"Good afternoon, everyone," Alex greeted, his voice projecting through the virtual meeting room. "As our organization continues to expand globally, the management of remote and distributed teams becomes increasingly crucial. Today, we'll explore strategies for effectively leading teams across borders and navigating the challenges of remote collaboration."

Embracing Virtual Collaboration Tools

Alex began by emphasizing the importance of embracing virtual collaboration tools to facilitate seamless communication and collaboration among remote teams.

"Technology bridges the gap," Alex noted. "By leveraging virtual collaboration tools such as video conferencing, project management software, and instant messaging platforms, we can overcome the barriers of distance and time zones and create a unified and connected team."

Establishing Clear Communication Channels

Next, Alex highlighted the importance of establishing clear communication channels and protocols to ensure that remote team members stay informed and engaged.

"Communication is key," Alex affirmed. "As leaders, we must establish clear communication channels and protocols to keep remote team members informed and engaged. Whether it's regular team meetings, status updates, or informal check-ins, effective communication is essential for building trust and fostering collaboration among remote teams."

Cultivating Trust and Accountability

Alex stressed the importance of cultivating trust and accountability within remote teams, recognizing that trust is the foundation of effective collaboration.

"Trust is earned," Alex declared. "As leaders, it's essential that we cultivate trust and accountability within our remote teams. By setting clear expectations, providing support and feedback, and recognizing and rewarding achievements, we can foster a culture of trust and accountability that drives success."

Navigating Time Zone Differences

Lastly, Alex addressed the challenge of navigating time zone differences and ensuring that remote team members feel included and supported.

"Time zones can be challenging," Alex acknowledged. "As leaders, we must be mindful of time zone differences and find creative solutions to ensure that remote team members feel included and supported. Whether it's scheduling flexible meetings, rotating meeting times to accommodate different time zones, or recording meetings for those unable to attend live, we must prioritize inclusivity and accessibility in our remote collaboration efforts."

Conclusion

As the virtual meeting came to a close, the leadership team left the collaboration hub with a deeper understanding of the complexities of managing remote and distributed teams. Inspired by Alex's insights, they were ready to embrace virtual collaboration tools, establish clear communication channels, cultivate trust and accountability, and navigate time zone differences as they continued to lead and empower their remote teams to achieve success in the global marketplace.

Adapting to Different Regulatory Environments

In the meticulously organized conference room of InovaTech's regulatory compliance department, Alex Carter stood before the leadership team, ready to delve into the complexities of adapting to different regulatory environments in global business operations. Today's focus: understanding the diverse regulatory landscapes across borders and navigating compliance challenges with agility and foresight.

Setting the Stage

"Good morning, everyone," Alex greeted, his voice resonating with authority and confidence. "As we expand our operations into new markets around the world, it's crucial that we navigate the diverse regulatory environments with precision and foresight. Today, we'll explore strategies for adapting to different regulatory landscapes and ensuring compliance across borders."

Understanding Regulatory Diversity

Alex began by emphasizing the importance of understanding the diversity of regulatory environments across different countries and regions.

"Regulatory landscapes vary," Alex noted. "Each country and region has its own set of laws, regulations, and compliance requirements governing business operations. As leaders, it's essential that we understand the nuances of these regulatory environments and adapt our strategies accordingly."

Prioritizing Compliance

Next, Alex highlighted the importance of prioritizing compliance and risk management in global business operations.

"Compliance is non-negotiable," Alex affirmed. "In today's interconnected world, compliance is essential for maintaining trust and credibility with customers, partners, and stakeholders. As leaders, we must prioritize compliance and ensure that our business operations adhere to the highest ethical and legal standards."

Investing in Regulatory Intelligence

Alex stressed the importance of investing in regulatory intelligence and staying informed about changes and updates in regulatory environments.

"Knowledge is power," Alex declared. "By investing in regulatory intelligence and staying informed about changes and updates in regulatory environments, we can anticipate compliance challenges and proactively adapt our strategies. Whether it's through regular training sessions, industry publications, or partnerships with regulatory experts, we must continuously seek to expand our knowledge and expertise."

Building Strategic Partnerships

Lastly, Alex addressed the importance of building strategic partnerships with local experts and stakeholders to navigate regulatory challenges effectively.

"Collaboration is key," Alex noted. "In unfamiliar regulatory environments, local expertise can be invaluable. As leaders, we must build strategic partnerships with local experts, consultants, and stakeholders who can provide insights and guidance on navigating regulatory challenges. By leveraging their knowledge and experience, we can ensure compliance and mitigate risks effectively."

Conclusion

As the discussion came to a close, the leadership team left the conference room with a renewed understanding of the importance of adapting to different regulatory environments in global business operations. Inspired by Alex's insights, they were ready to prioritize compliance, invest in regulatory intelligence, and build strategic partnerships as they continued to expand and thrive in the global marketplace.

Case Studies of Global Innovative Leaders

In the innovation hub of InovaTech's headquarters, Alex Carter stood before the leadership team, ready to showcase real-life examples of global innovative leaders who have successfully navigated the complexities of leading in the global arena. Today's focus: examining the strategies and practices of renowned leaders who have achieved success on the global stage.

Setting the Stage

"Good afternoon, everyone," Alex greeted, his voice filled with anticipation. "Today, we have the opportunity to learn from some of the most influential leaders in the global business world. These case studies offer valuable insights into the leadership strategies and practices that have propelled these individuals and their organizations to success."

Case Study 1: Satya Nadella, CEO of Microsoft

Alex began by sharing the story of Satya Nadella, CEO of Microsoft, who has been widely recognized for his transformative leadership in guiding Microsoft's evolution into a cloud-based, AI-driven company.

"Satya Nadella is a visionary leader," Alex noted. "Under his leadership, Microsoft has undergone a remarkable transformation, embracing innovation and leveraging emerging technologies to drive growth and competitiveness. Nadella's emphasis on empathy, curiosity, and continuous learning has fostered a culture of innovation within Microsoft, empowering employees to explore new ideas and pursue bold initiatives."

Case Study 2: Mary Barra, CEO of General Motors

Next, Alex highlighted the achievements of Mary Barra, CEO of General Motors, who has been instrumental in leading the company's transition to electric and autonomous vehicles and championing diversity and inclusion in the automotive industry.

"Mary Barra is a trailblazer," Alex affirmed. "Her strategic vision and bold leadership have positioned General Motors as a leader in the future of mobility. Barra's commitment to innovation, sustainability, and diversity has not only driven business success but also established General Motors as a purpose-driven organization that is shaping the future of transportation."

Case Study 3: Elon Musk, CEO of Tesla and SpaceX

Lastly, Alex shared the story of Elon Musk, CEO of Tesla and SpaceX, whose visionary leadership and ambitious goals have revolutionized the automotive and aerospace industries.

"Elon Musk is a visionary disruptor," Alex declared. "Through his relentless pursuit of innovation and his willingness to take bold risks, Musk has redefined what is possible in both the automotive and aerospace industries. His audacious goals, such as colonizing Mars and accelerating the transition to sustainable energy, have inspired millions and propelled Tesla and SpaceX to the forefront of technological innovation."

Conclusion

As the presentation came to a close, the leadership team left the innovation hub feeling inspired and invigorated by the stories of global innovative leaders. They were reminded of the importance of visionary leadership, strategic foresight, and a commitment to innovation in navigating the challenges of leading in the global arena. Armed with valuable insights from these case studies, they were ready to apply these lessons to their own leadership journey as they continued to drive innovation and success within InovaTech.

9

Chapter 9: Ethical Leadership in a Rapidly Changing World

Defining Ethical Leadership

In the serene ambiance of InovaTech's ethics and compliance office, Alex Carter stood before the leadership team, poised to explore the critical importance of ethical leadership in today's rapidly changing world. Today's focus: defining the principles and values that underpin ethical leadership and guide decision-making in complex and evolving environments.

Setting the Stage

"Good morning, everyone," Alex greeted, his tone firm yet approachable. "As leaders, we bear a profound responsibility to uphold the highest ethical standards and lead with integrity, especially in times of change and uncertainty. Today, we'll delve into the essence of ethical leadership and explore how it shapes our actions and decisions in a rapidly changing world."

The Essence of Ethical Leadership

Alex began by emphasizing the fundamental principles of ethical leadership, rooted in honesty, integrity, and accountability.

"At its core, ethical leadership is about doing the right thing, even when no one is watching," Alex explained. "It's about upholding honesty, integrity, and transparency in all our interactions and decisions. Ethical leaders demonstrate a commitment to fairness, respect, and justice, and they hold themselves and others accountable for their actions."

Guiding Principles

Next, Alex outlined the guiding principles that define ethical leadership and serve as a compass for navigating moral dilemmas and ethical challenges.

"Ethical leaders adhere to a set of guiding principles that inform their decisions and actions," Alex noted. "These principles include honesty, integrity, fairness, respect, and empathy. Ethical leaders prioritize the well-being of their stakeholders and seek to create a positive impact on society while upholding the highest ethical standards."

Leading by Example

Alex stressed the importance of leading by example and setting a positive tone from the top, recognizing that ethical leadership starts with personal integrity and accountability.

"As leaders, we must lead by example," Alex affirmed. "Our

actions speak louder than words, and we must demonstrate integrity, honesty, and ethical behavior in everything we do. By setting a positive example and holding ourselves to the highest ethical standards, we inspire trust and confidence in our teams and foster a culture of ethics and accountability."

Conclusion

As the discussion came to a close, the leadership team left the ethics and compliance office with a renewed commitment to ethical leadership. Inspired by Alex's insights, they were ready to embrace the principles of honesty, integrity, and accountability in their leadership roles and uphold the highest ethical standards as they navigated the challenges of a rapidly changing world.

Balancing Profit with Purpose

In the tranquil ambiance of InovaTech's executive boardroom, Alex Carter stood before the leadership team, prepared to navigate the delicate balance between profit-seeking and purpose-driven leadership. Today's focus: exploring how ethical leaders can reconcile the pursuit of financial success with a commitment to social responsibility and ethical conduct.

Setting the Stage

"Good afternoon, everyone," Alex greeted, his demeanor poised and attentive. "As leaders, we face the ongoing challenge of balancing the pursuit of profit with a deeper sense of purpose and social responsibility. Today, we'll delve into the complexities of this balancing act and explore strategies for leading with integrity while driving financial success."

The Challenge of Balancing Priorities

Alex began by acknowledging the inherent tension between profit-seeking and purpose-driven leadership, recognizing that ethical leaders must navigate this challenge with care and foresight.

"Balancing profit with purpose is no easy task," Alex acknowledged. "In a competitive business environment driven by financial metrics and shareholder expectations, it can be tempting to prioritize short-term gains over long-term sustainability and social impact. However, ethical leaders recognize that true success lies in finding a harmonious balance between financial performance and ethical conduct."

Aligning Business Goals with Social Impact

Next, Alex emphasized the importance of aligning business goals with social impact and leveraging the power of business as a force for positive change.

"Businesses have a unique opportunity to drive social change and make a meaningful impact on society," Alex noted. "Ethical leaders recognize that profit and purpose are not mutually exclusive; rather, they are interconnected and mutually reinforcing. By aligning business goals with social impact initiatives, organizations can create shared value for all stakeholders and contribute to the greater good while driving financial success."

Prioritizing Stakeholder Well-Being

Alex stressed the importance of prioritizing the well-being of all stakeholders, including employees, customers, suppliers, and the community at large.

"Stakeholder well-being is paramount," Alex affirmed. "Ethical leaders prioritize the interests of all stakeholders, not just shareholders. They recognize that sustainable business practices, ethical conduct, and social responsibility are essential for building trust, fostering loyalty, and driving long-term success. By putting people first and prioritizing stakeholder well-being, organizations can create a positive impact on society while delivering value to shareholders."

Conclusion

As the discussion came to a close, the leadership team left the executive boardroom with a deeper appreciation for the complexities of balancing profit with purpose in ethical leadership. Inspired by Alex's insights, they were ready to embrace the challenge of leading with integrity while driving financial success, recognizing that by aligning business goals with social impact and prioritizing stakeholder well-being, they could create a more sustainable and ethical future for InovaTech and the communities they serve.

Navigating Ethical Dilemmas in Innovation

In the contemplative atmosphere of InovaTech's innovation lab, Alex Carter stood before the leadership team, ready to explore the ethical complexities inherent in the pursuit of innovation. Today's focus: navigating the ethical dilemmas that arise in the process of driving technological advancements and transformative change.

Setting the Stage

"Good morning, everyone," Alex greeted, his voice echoing in the spacious lab. "Innovation is the lifeblood of our organization, driving growth, competitiveness, and progress. However, with innovation comes ethical responsibility. Today, we'll delve into the ethical dilemmas that accompany innovation and explore strategies for making ethical decisions in a rapidly changing world."

The Intersection of Innovation and Ethics

Alex began by highlighting the intersection of innovation and ethics, recognizing that technological advancements can have profound ethical implications.

"Innovation is not morally neutral," Alex affirmed. "Technological advancements can have far-reaching consequences for individuals, communities, and society as a whole. As leaders, it's essential that we consider the ethical implications of our innovations and strive to ensure that our technological advancements are aligned with our values and principles."

Anticipating Ethical Challenges

Next, Alex emphasized the importance of proactively identifying and addressing potential ethical challenges before they escalate into crises.

"Prevention is better than cure," Alex noted. "Ethical leaders anticipate ethical dilemmas and proactively implement measures to mitigate risks and uphold ethical standards. Whether it's through ethical impact assessments, stakeholder consultations, or ethical training programs, we must be vigilant in identifying and addressing potential ethical challenges before they compromise our integrity and reputation."

Ethical Decision-Making Frameworks

Alex introduced various ethical decision-making frameworks that can guide leaders in navigating complex ethical dilemmas, such as utilitarianism, deontology, and virtue ethics.

"Ethical decision-making is a complex process," Alex explained. "By utilizing ethical frameworks and principles, we can systematically evaluate the ethical implications of our actions and make informed decisions that prioritize the greater good. Whether it's considering the consequences of our actions, adhering to moral principles, or cultivating virtuous character traits, ethical decision-making frameworks provide valuable guidance in navigating ethical dilemmas."

Fostering a Culture of Ethics

Lastly, Alex emphasized the importance of fostering a culture of ethics within the organization, where ethical considerations are integrated into every aspect of decision-making and behavior.

"Culture is key," Alex affirmed. "Ethical leaders cultivate a culture of ethics where integrity, honesty, and accountability are not just ideals but lived values. By fostering open dialogue, encouraging ethical reflection, and recognizing and rewarding ethical behavior, we can create a workplace where ethical considerations are embedded into the fabric of our organizational culture."

Conclusion

As the discussion came to a close, the leadership team left the innovation lab with a renewed commitment to ethical leadership in innovation. Inspired by Alex's insights, they were ready to navigate the ethical complexities of driving innovation, proactively address ethical challenges, and foster a culture of ethics within InovaTech, ensuring that their technological advancements were not only innovative but also ethical and responsible.

Building Trust and Credibility

In the serene ambiance of InovaTech's executive boardroom, Alex Carter stood before the leadership team, poised to explore the indispensable role of trust and credibility in ethical leadership. Today's focus: understanding how ethical leaders build and maintain trust with stakeholders in a rapidly changing world.

Setting the Stage

"Good afternoon, everyone," Alex greeted, his tone earnest and sincere. "Trust is the foundation of leadership. In today's fast-paced and interconnected world, building and maintaining trust is more important than ever. Today, we'll delve into the strategies and practices that ethical leaders employ to earn the trust and credibility of their stakeholders."

The Importance of Trust

Alex began by emphasizing the critical importance of trust in leadership, recognizing that trust is the bedrock upon which strong relationships and successful organizations are built.

"Trust is the currency of leadership," Alex affirmed. "Without trust, leaders cannot effectively inspire, influence, or lead. Ethical leaders understand that trust is earned through consistent actions, transparency, and integrity. They recognize that trust is fragile and must be nurtured and safeguarded at all times."

Transparency and Open Communication

Next, Alex highlighted the importance of transparency and open communication in building trust with stakeholders.

"Transparency breeds trust," Alex noted. "Ethical leaders are transparent in their actions and decisions, communicating openly and honestly with stakeholders. They share information proactively, address concerns and questions openly, and seek feedback and input from stakeholders. By fostering transparency and open communication, leaders demonstrate their commitment to integrity and build trust with their teams, customers, and partners."

Consistency and Reliability

Alex stressed the importance of consistency and reliability in building trust over time.

"Consistency builds credibility," Alex declared. "Ethical leaders are consistent in their words and actions, aligning their behaviors with their values and principles. They follow through on their commitments, deliver on their promises, and uphold their obligations to stakeholders. By demonstrating reliability and consistency, leaders earn the trust and confidence of their teams and stakeholders."

Integrity and Authenticity

Lastly, Alex emphasized the importance of integrity and authenticity in building trust and credibility as a leader.

"Integrity is non-negotiable," Alex affirmed. "Ethical leaders act with integrity, aligning their actions with their values and principles. They are authentic and genuine in their interactions, demonstrating sincerity, humility, and vulnerability. By leading with integrity and authenticity, leaders inspire trust and loyalty among their teams and stakeholders."

Conclusion

As the discussion came to a close, the leadership team left the executive boardroom with a deeper appreciation for the indispensable role of trust and credibility in ethical leadership. Inspired by Alex's insights, they were ready to prioritize transparency, consistency, integrity, and authenticity in their leadership roles, recognizing that by building and maintaining trust with their teams, customers, and partners, they could lead with confidence and make a positive impact in a rapidly changing world.

Social Responsibility and Sustainability

In the socially conscious atmosphere of InovaTech's sustainability department, Alex Carter stood before the leadership team, prepared to explore the critical role of social responsibility and sustainability in ethical leadership. Today's focus: understanding how ethical leaders integrate social responsibility and sustainability into their organizational practices and decision-making.

Setting the Stage

"Good morning, everyone," Alex greeted, his voice resonating with purpose. "As leaders, we have a responsibility not only to our shareholders but also to society and the planet. Today, we'll delve into the principles of social responsibility and sustainability and explore how they intersect with ethical leadership in a rapidly changing world."

Embracing Social Responsibility

Alex began by emphasizing the importance of embracing social responsibility as a core component of ethical leadership.

"Social responsibility is at the heart of ethical leadership," Alex affirmed. "Ethical leaders recognize that their organizations have a broader impact on society and must act in the best interests of all stakeholders, including employees, customers, communities, and the environment. By embracing social responsibility, leaders demonstrate their commitment to making a positive difference in the world."

Integrating Sustainability Practices

Next, Alex highlighted the importance of integrating sustainability practices into organizational operations and decision-making.

"Sustainability is essential for long-term success," Alex noted. "Ethical leaders understand that sustainable practices are not only good for the planet but also good for business. They prioritize environmental stewardship, resource conservation, and climate action, integrating sustainability into every aspect of their organization's strategy, operations, and culture."

Corporate Citizenship and Community Engagement

Alex stressed the importance of corporate citizenship and community engagement in demonstrating social responsibility.

"Corporate citizenship is about giving back to the communities we serve," Alex declared. "Ethical leaders engage with their communities, support local initiatives, and contribute to social causes that align with their organizational values and mission. By being good corporate citizens, leaders build trust, enhance reputation, and create shared value for society and the organization."

Aligning Profit with Purpose

Lastly, Alex emphasized the importance of aligning profit with purpose and leveraging business as a force for positive change.

"Profit and purpose are not mutually exclusive," Alex affirmed. "Ethical leaders recognize that by aligning business goals with societal needs and environmental stewardship, organizations can create shared value for all stakeholders. By pursuing profit with purpose, leaders demonstrate their commitment to making a meaningful impact on society while driving long-term success for their organizations."

Conclusion

As the discussion came to a close, the leadership team left the sustainability department with a renewed commitment to social responsibility and sustainability in ethical leadership. Inspired by Alex's insights, they were ready to integrate sustainability practices, engage with their communities, and align profit with purpose as they led InovaTech forward in a rapidly changing world, ensuring that their actions reflected their commitment to making a positive difference in society and the planet.

Ethical Decision-Making Frameworks

In the contemplative atmosphere of InovaTech's ethics and compliance office, Alex Carter stood before the leadership team, poised to explore the essential role of ethical decision-making frameworks in guiding leaders through complex moral dilemmas. Today's focus: understanding the various ethical frameworks that can help leaders navigate ethical challenges with clarity and integrity.

Setting the Stage

"Good afternoon, everyone," Alex greeted, his tone measured and composed. "Ethical decision-making is a cornerstone of effective leadership. In today's rapidly changing world, leaders are confronted with increasingly complex moral dilemmas that require careful consideration and ethical reflection. Today, we'll explore the ethical decision-making frameworks that can assist us in navigating these challenges with wisdom and integrity."

Utilitarianism: Maximizing Utility

Alex began by introducing utilitarianism, a consequentialist ethical framework that evaluates the moral worth of actions based on their outcomes and consequences.

"Utilitarianism focuses on maximizing utility," Alex explained. "According to this framework, the morally right action is the one that produces the greatest overall happiness or well-being for the greatest number of people. When faced with an ethical dilemma, leaders employing a utilitarian approach consider the potential outcomes of each course of action and choose the option that maximizes the overall good."

Deontology: Upholding Moral Duties

Next, Alex introduced deontology, a non-consequentialist ethical framework that emphasizes the importance of moral duties and principles in guiding ethical decision-making.

"Deontology prioritizes moral duties and principles," Alex noted. "According to this framework, certain actions are inherently right or wrong, regardless of their consequences. Leaders employing a deontological approach focus on upholding moral duties and principles, such as honesty, fairness, and respect for human dignity, and make decisions based on their adherence to these fundamental ethical norms."

Virtue Ethics: Cultivating Virtuous Character

Alex then discussed virtue ethics, an ethical framework that emphasizes the cultivation of virtuous character traits and personal integrity.

"Virtue ethics emphasizes the importance of character," Alex affirmed. "According to this framework, ethical behavior stems from the cultivation of virtuous character traits, such as honesty, courage, compassion, and integrity. Leaders employing a virtue ethics approach prioritize the development of these character traits within themselves and their teams, recognizing that ethical decision-making flows naturally from virtuous character."

Integrating Ethical Frameworks

Lastly, Alex emphasized the importance of integrating multiple ethical frameworks and considering a range of perspectives when navigating complex ethical dilemmas.

"No single ethical framework provides all the answers," Alex concluded. "Effective ethical decision-making requires a holistic approach that integrates insights from multiple ethical perspectives. By considering a range of ethical frameworks and perspectives, leaders can make informed, nuanced, and ethically sound decisions that prioritize integrity, fairness, and the well-being of all stakeholders."

Conclusion

As the discussion came to a close, the leadership team left the ethics and compliance office with a deeper understanding of the various ethical decision-making frameworks that can guide them through complex moral dilemmas. Inspired by Alex's insights, they were ready to integrate these frameworks into their leadership practices, ensuring that their decisions reflected a commitment to integrity, fairness, and ethical conduct in a rapidly changing world.

10

Chapter 10: The Future of Leadership: Trends and Predictions

Emerging Trends in Leadership and Innovation

In the forward-thinking atmosphere of InovaTech's innovation lab, Alex Carter stood before the leadership team, prepared to explore the dynamic landscape of future leadership trends and innovations. Today's focus: uncovering the emerging trends that will shape the future of leadership in a rapidly evolving world.

Setting the Stage

"Good morning, everyone," Alex greeted, his voice filled with anticipation. "As leaders, we must constantly adapt and evolve to meet the challenges and opportunities of an ever-changing world. Today, we'll explore the emerging trends in leadership and innovation that will define the future of our organizations and industries."

Embracing Digital Transformation

Alex began by highlighting the transformative impact of digital technologies on leadership practices and organizational dynamics.

"Digital transformation is revolutionizing the way we lead and innovate," Alex noted. "From AI and machine learning to data analytics and automation, digital technologies are reshaping how we collaborate, communicate, and make decisions. Leaders must embrace these technologies and leverage them to drive innovation, agility, and competitiveness in their organizations."

Empowering Remote and Distributed Teams

Next, Alex discussed the rise of remote and distributed work models and their implications for leadership and organizational culture.

"The future of work is remote and distributed," Alex affirmed. "Advancements in communication technologies and changing workforce preferences are enabling more flexible and remote work arrangements. Leaders must adapt to leading teams across geographical boundaries, fostering collaboration, and maintaining a strong sense of connection and belonging among remote employees."

Cultivating Diversity and Inclusion

Alex emphasized the importance of cultivating diversity and inclusion in leadership and organizational practices.

"Diversity is a strength," Alex declared. "Leaders must prioritize diversity and inclusion, not only as a moral imperative but also as a strategic advantage. Diverse teams bring a wide range of perspectives, experiences, and ideas to the table, driving innovation, creativity, and resilience. By fostering a culture of diversity and inclusion, leaders can create a more dynamic and adaptive organization."

Nurturing Agile and Adaptive Leadership

Lastly, Alex discussed the growing importance of agile and adaptive leadership in navigating uncertainty and complexity.

"Agility is essential," Alex affirmed. "In a rapidly changing world, leaders must be agile, adaptable, and resilient. They must embrace uncertainty, experiment with new approaches, and pivot quickly in response to changing market dynamics and customer needs. By nurturing agile and adaptive leadership practices, leaders can steer their organizations through turbulent times and emerge stronger and more resilient."

Conclusion

As the discussion came to a close, the leadership team left the innovation lab with a renewed understanding of the emerging trends that will shape the future of leadership. Inspired by Alex's insights, they were ready to embrace digital transformation, empower remote teams, cultivate diversity and inclusion, and nurture agile and adaptive leadership practices as they led InovaTech into the future, prepared to navigate the challenges and opportunities of a rapidly evolving world.

CHAPTER 10: THE FUTURE OF LEADERSHIP: TRENDS AND PREDICTIONS

The Impact of Artificial Intelligence on Leadership

In the innovative atmosphere of InovaTech's research and development center, Alex Carter stood before the leadership team, ready to delve into the transformative impact of artificial intelligence (AI) on the future of leadership. Today's focus: exploring how AI is reshaping leadership practices and organizational dynamics in unprecedented ways.

Setting the Stage

"Good afternoon, everyone," Alex greeted, his voice filled with energy and enthusiasm. "Artificial intelligence is revolutionizing the way we work, communicate, and lead. Today, we'll explore the profound impact of AI on leadership and uncover how it is reshaping the future of our organizations and industries."

Harnessing AI for Decision-Making

Alex began by highlighting the role of AI in augmenting decision-making processes and enhancing leadership effectiveness.

"AI is a game-changer for decision-making," Alex noted. "From predictive analytics and data-driven insights to intelligent automation and cognitive computing, AI technologies empower leaders to make faster, more informed decisions based on real-time data and analysis. By harnessing the power of AI, leaders can gain deeper insights, identify trends and patterns, and anticipate future opportunities and challenges with greater accuracy and confidence."

Personalizing Leadership and Employee Experience

Next, Alex discussed the potential of AI to personalize leadership approaches and employee experiences, fostering a more engaging and inclusive workplace culture.

"AI enables personalized leadership," Alex affirmed. "By leveraging AI-powered tools, leaders can tailor their leadership styles and communication strategies to individual preferences, strengths, and needs. AI also allows for personalized employee experiences, from customized learning and development programs to personalized feedback and recognition. By harnessing AI to personalize leadership and employee experiences, organizations can foster a more supportive, inclusive, and engaging workplace culture."

Augmenting Human Capabilities

Alex emphasized the importance of viewing AI as a complement to human capabilities rather than a replacement.

"AI augments human potential," Alex declared. "While AI has the potential to automate routine tasks and processes, its true value lies in augmenting human capabilities and freeing up time for higher-order thinking, creativity, and innovation. Leaders must embrace AI as a tool to enhance, rather than replace, human intelligence and creativity. By leveraging AI to augment human capabilities, leaders can unlock new levels of productivity, efficiency, and innovation in their organizations."

Mitigating Ethical and Bias Risks

Lastly, Alex discussed the importance of mitigating ethical and bias risks associated with AI deployment in leadership contexts.

"Ethical considerations are paramount," Alex affirmed. "As AI becomes increasingly integrated into leadership practices, it's essential to mitigate ethical risks, such as privacy concerns, data security, and algorithmic bias. Leaders must ensure that AI systems are designed and deployed responsibly, with careful attention to fairness, transparency, and accountability. By prioritizing ethical AI practices, leaders can build trust, minimize risks, and maximize the positive impact of AI on leadership and organizational performance."

Conclusion

As the discussion came to a close, the leadership team left the research and development center with a deeper understanding of the transformative impact of artificial intelligence on the future of leadership. Inspired by Alex's insights, they were ready to embrace AI as a tool to enhance decision-making, personalize leadership approaches, augment human capabilities, and mitigate ethical risks, prepared to lead InovaTech into a future where AI and human intelligence work hand in hand to drive innovation, growth, and success.

The Future Workplace: Preparing for Change

In the dynamic atmosphere of InovaTech's innovation hub, Alex Carter stood before the leadership team, poised to explore the evolving landscape of the future workplace. Today's focus: preparing for the transformative changes that will redefine how we work, collaborate, and lead in the years to come.

Setting the Stage

"Good morning, everyone," Alex greeted, his voice echoing with anticipation. "The future of work is upon us, and it promises to be both exciting and challenging. Today, we'll explore the emerging trends and shifts that will shape the future workplace and discuss how we can prepare ourselves and our organizations for the changes ahead."

Embracing Flexibility and Remote Work

Alex began by discussing the rise of flexibility and remote work as central features of the future workplace.

"Flexibility is the new norm," Alex noted. "Advancements in technology and changing workforce preferences are driving a shift towards flexible work arrangements, including remote work and hybrid models. Leaders must embrace this trend, providing the necessary infrastructure and support to enable employees to work from anywhere while maintaining productivity, collaboration, and engagement."

Redefining Collaboration and Communication

Next, Alex emphasized the importance of redefining collaboration and communication in the future workplace.

"Collaboration is evolving," Alex affirmed. "As remote and distributed work becomes more prevalent, leaders must reimagine how teams collaborate and communicate. Virtual collaboration tools, digital platforms, and immersive technologies offer new opportunities for remote teams to collaborate effectively and foster innovation. Leaders must leverage these tools to create seamless and inclusive collaboration experiences across geographical boundaries."

Prioritizing Well-Being and Work-Life Balance

Alex discussed the growing emphasis on well-being and work-life balance in the future workplace.

"Well-being is paramount," Alex declared. "In a world of constant connectivity and digital overload, leaders must prioritize the well-being and mental health of their employees. Flexible work arrangements, wellness programs, and supportive policies can help employees achieve a healthier work-life balance and maintain overall well-being. By prioritizing employee well-being, leaders can enhance engagement, retention, and organizational performance."

Embracing Lifelong Learning and Skills Development

Lastly, Alex emphasized the importance of embracing lifelong learning and skills development in the future workplace.

"Learning is continuous," Alex noted. "In a rapidly changing world, leaders must foster a culture of continuous learning and skills development to adapt to evolving job roles and industry trends. Investing in employee training, upskilling, and reskilling initiatives can help employees stay ahead of the curve and thrive in the future workplace. By prioritizing learning and development, leaders can build a more agile, resilient, and future-ready workforce."

Conclusion

As the discussion came to a close, the leadership team left the innovation hub with a deeper understanding of the transformative changes that await the future workplace. Inspired by Alex's insights, they were ready to embrace flexibility, redefine collaboration, prioritize well-being, and foster a culture of lifelong learning in their organizations, prepared to lead InovaTech into a future where the workplace is dynamic, inclusive, and adaptable to the needs of employees and the demands of a rapidly changing world.

Lifelong Learning: Staying Relevant in a Fast-Paced World

In the vibrant atmosphere of InovaTech's innovation center, Alex Carter stood before the leadership team, ready to explore the imperative of lifelong learning in navigating the fast-paced landscape of the future. Today's focus: understanding how continuous learning is essential for staying relevant and thriving in a rapidly evolving world.

Setting the Stage

"Good afternoon, everyone," Alex greeted, his voice resonating with conviction. "In the ever-evolving landscape of the future, one thing remains constant: the need for continuous learning and skills development. Today, we'll delve into the importance of lifelong learning and discuss how it is crucial for staying relevant and thriving in a fast-paced world."

Embracing a Growth Mindset

Alex began by emphasizing the importance of adopting a growth mindset as the foundation for lifelong learning.

"A growth mindset is key," Alex affirmed. "In a world of constant change and disruption, leaders must embrace a mindset of continuous growth and development. By adopting a growth mindset, individuals are open to new challenges, see failure as an opportunity for learning, and actively seek out opportunities to expand their knowledge and skills."

Nurturing Curiosity and Exploration

Next, Alex discussed the importance of nurturing curiosity and exploration as drivers of lifelong learning.

"Curiosity fuels learning," Alex noted. "Curious individuals are naturally inclined to explore new ideas, ask questions, and seek out new experiences. Leaders must cultivate a culture of curiosity within their organizations, encouraging employees to pursue their interests, experiment with new approaches, and embrace lifelong learning as a journey of discovery."

Embracing Technology and Innovation

Alex emphasized the role of technology and innovation in enabling lifelong learning opportunities.

"Technology is a game-changer," Alex declared. "Advancements in digital learning platforms, online courses, and virtual reality simulations have democratized access to education and made lifelong learning more accessible and convenient than ever before. Leaders must leverage these technologies to provide employees with personalized learning experiences and empower them to acquire new skills and knowledge at their own pace."

Fostering a Learning Culture

Lastly, Alex discussed the importance of fostering a learning culture within organizations to support lifelong learning initiatives.

"Culture is critical," Alex affirmed. "Leaders must create an environment where learning is valued, celebrated, and integrated into every aspect of the organization. By fostering a learning culture that encourages continuous growth and development, leaders can unleash the full potential of their teams and ensure that their organizations remain agile, innovative, and competitive in a fast-paced world."

Conclusion

As the discussion came to a close, the leadership team left the innovation center with a renewed commitment to lifelong learning as the cornerstone of success in the future. Inspired by

Alex's insights, they were ready to embrace a growth mindset, nurture curiosity and exploration, leverage technology and innovation, and foster a learning culture within their organizations, prepared to lead InovaTech into a future where learning is continuous, opportunities abound, and success knows no bounds.

Predictions for the Next Decade of Leadership

In the innovative ambiance of InovaTech's strategy room, Alex Carter stood before the leadership team, ready to unveil his predictions for the next decade of leadership. Today's focus: forecasting the trends and shifts that will shape the future of leadership in the years to come.

Setting the Stage

"Good morning, everyone," Alex greeted, his voice carrying a sense of anticipation. "As we stand on the brink of a new decade, it's essential to look ahead and anticipate the trends that will redefine the landscape of leadership. Today, I'll share my predictions for the next decade of leadership and discuss how we can prepare ourselves and our organizations for the challenges and opportunities that lie ahead."

Embracing Adaptive Leadership

Alex began by predicting a growing emphasis on adaptive leadership in the face of increasing uncertainty and complexity.

"Adaptability will be paramount," Alex affirmed. "Leaders must be agile, resilient, and able to navigate ambiguity and change with confidence. Adaptive leadership, characterized by the ability to anticipate, respond to, and learn from disruptions, will become increasingly essential in a world where the only constant is change."

Prioritizing Purpose-Driven Leadership

Next, Alex forecasted a shift towards purpose-driven leadership, where leaders prioritize values, ethics, and social responsibility.

"Purpose will drive leadership," Alex noted. "In an age of heightened social consciousness and environmental awareness, leaders must align their organizations with a higher purpose beyond profit. Purpose-driven leadership, characterized by a commitment to making a positive impact on society and the planet, will become a defining trait of successful leaders in the next decade."

Harnessing the Power of Diversity and Inclusion

Alex emphasized the transformative potential of diversity and inclusion in driving innovation and fostering organizational success.

"Diversity will be a strength," Alex declared. "Leaders must embrace diversity and inclusion as strategic imperatives, recognizing the value of diverse perspectives, backgrounds, and experiences in driving innovation, creativity, and resilience. In the next decade, organizations that prioritize diversity and inclusion will outperform their peers and lead the way in shaping a more equitable and inclusive world."

Embracing Technological Advancements

Lastly, Alex predicted a continued reliance on technology and innovation as drivers of organizational success.

"Technology will redefine leadership," Alex affirmed. "As advancements in artificial intelligence, automation, and digital transformation accelerate, leaders must adapt to new ways of working and leading in a technology-driven world. Those who embrace technology and leverage it to enhance decision-making, collaboration, and customer experiences will gain a competitive edge and lead their organizations to new heights of success."

Conclusion

As the discussion came to a close, the leadership team left the strategy room with a renewed sense of purpose and determination. Inspired by Alex's predictions, they were ready to embrace adaptive leadership, prioritize purpose-driven values, harness the power of diversity and inclusion, and leverage technology and innovation to lead InovaTech into a future where leadership knows no bounds and success knows no limits.

Action Plan: Implementing Innovative Leadership Practices

In the strategic ambiance of InovaTech's boardroom, Alex Carter stood before the leadership team, poised to outline an action plan for implementing innovative leadership practices in the organization. Today's focus: translating insights and predictions into tangible strategies and initiatives that will drive success in the future.

Setting the Stage

"Good afternoon, everyone," Alex greeted, his tone infused with determination. "As we look ahead to the future of leadership, it's crucial to turn our insights and predictions into action. Today, I'll outline an action plan for implementing innovative leadership practices that will position us for success in the years to come."

Embracing Change and Adaptability

Alex began by emphasizing the importance of embracing change and fostering adaptability within the organization.

"Change is inevitable," Alex affirmed. "To thrive in the future, we must embrace change and cultivate adaptability at all levels of the organization. This means fostering a culture that values experimentation, resilience, and continuous learning, where employees feel empowered to adapt and innovate in response to evolving challenges and opportunities."

Aligning with Purpose and Values

Next, Alex discussed the importance of aligning leadership practices with the organization's purpose and values.

"Our purpose guides us," Alex noted. "To lead with impact, we must align our actions with our purpose and values, ensuring that every decision we make reflects our commitment to making a positive difference in the world. This means embedding purpose-driven leadership practices into our organizational culture, where every employee feels connected to our mission and motivated to contribute to our collective success."

Investing in Diversity and Inclusion

Alex emphasized the transformative potential of investing in diversity and inclusion initiatives.

"Diversity drives innovation," Alex declared. "To unlock our full potential, we must invest in diversity and inclusion initiatives that foster a culture of belonging, where every voice is heard, valued, and respected. This means implementing recruitment and retention strategies that prioritize diversity, providing training and development programs that promote inclusion, and holding ourselves accountable for creating an environment where everyone can thrive."

Leveraging Technology and Innovation

Lastly, Alex discussed the importance of leveraging technology and innovation to drive organizational success.

"Technology is our ally," Alex affirmed. "To stay ahead of

the curve, we must embrace technology and innovation as enablers of growth and efficiency. This means investing in digital transformation initiatives that enhance our capabilities, leveraging data and analytics to inform our decision-making, and exploring emerging technologies that have the potential to revolutionize our industry."

Conclusion

As the discussion came to a close, the leadership team left the boardroom with a clear vision and actionable plan for implementing innovative leadership practices in the organization. Inspired by Alex's guidance, they were ready to embrace change, align with purpose and values, invest in diversity and inclusion, and leverage technology and innovation to lead InovaTech into a future where success knows no bounds and leadership knows no limits.

About the Author

Goodson Mumba is a multifaceted individual known for his diverse expertise and prolific contributions across various fields. As an infopreneur, thought leader, and spiritual leader, he has inspired countless individuals through his insightful teachings and impactful writings. Mumba is also an accomplished author, with several notable works to his name, including "Understanding Corporate Worship," "The Years I Spent in a Week," "Management By Harmony," "The CEO's Diary," "Change to Change" and "Creative Thinking for results" His literary works span topics ranging from business management to personal development and spirituality, reflecting his broad range of interests and insights.

With a Master of Business Leadership (MBL) and a Bachelor of Arts in Theology (BTh), Mumba brings a unique blend of business acumen and spiritual wisdom to his work. His educational background is further enriched by a Group Diploma in Management Studies, providing him with a solid foundation in organizational dynamics and leadership principles. Additionally, Mumba holds diplomas in Education Psychology,

Leadership and Management Styles, Organizational Behaviour, Financial Accounting, Economic Growth and Development, and Project Management, showcasing his commitment to continuous learning and professional development.

Mumba's expertise extends beyond traditional academic disciplines, encompassing areas such as Neuro-Linguistic Programming (NLP) and Positive Psychology. His diverse skill set is complemented by a range of certifications, including Creative Problem Solving and Decision Making, Life Coaching Fundamentals and Techniques, Professional Life Coaching, and Performance Management System Design. These certifications reflect Mumba's dedication to equipping himself with the tools and knowledge necessary to empower others and drive positive change.

As an author, Mumba's writings reflect his deep understanding of human nature, organizational dynamics, and spiritual principles. His works offer practical insights, actionable strategies, and inspirational guidance for individuals seeking personal growth, professional success, and spiritual fulfillment. Mumba's holistic approach to life and leadership resonates with readers worldwide, making him a respected figure in both the business and spiritual communities.

Overall, Goodson Mumba's diverse background, extensive knowledge, and profound insights make him a sought-after speaker, mentor, and author. His commitment to excellence, lifelong learning, and service to others continues to inspire individuals to unlock their full potential and lead lives of purpose and significance.

Goodson Mumba is renowned for initiating the concept of Management by Harmony, revolutionizing traditional management practices with a focus on balanced and holistic approaches. He has authored two influential books on this subject: "Introduction to Management by Harmony" and its sequel, "Management by Harmony."

Mumba's work has significantly impacted the field, offering innovative strategies for fostering organizational harmony and efficiency. His contributions continue to shape contemporary management theories and practices.

www.ingramcontent.com/pod-product-compliance
Lightning Source LLC
Chambersburg PA
CBHW071828210526
45479CB00001B/42